★ CHAEL ★
SONNEN

THE VOICE *of* REASON
A VIP PASS TO ENLIGHTENMENT

First Published in 2012 by Victory Belt Publishing Inc.

ISBN 13: 978-1-936608-54-6

Printed in The United States

Table *of* Contents

Foreword
By JESUS CHRIST
Son of God
Savior of Humanity
COO, the Universe

*A*s you might imagine, I get contacted quite often by people requesting things, and the requests range from the mundane to the outlandish. I tend not to respond too frequently; when I do, I try to make my interest and involvement not only utilitarian but also as opaque as possible to avoid inviting even more requests, which my schedule would render impossible to address. Think Santa Claus has it tough? Imagine adding to his list of demanding customers the Jehovah's Witnesses and pretty much anyone else with any religious affiliation who's about to die and wants to be sure all his bases are covered.

I do my best to keep you informed by placing learned men like Galileo, Copernicus, and Kepler among you, but quite honestly, there seems to be no way to disabuse you of the collective notion that you are the center of the universe, and therefore worthy of my constant attention and intervention. Knowing what I know, I feel I can be blunt about this: You are not the center of the universe. There are momentary exceptions, of course—Ben Hogan in 1953, Jim Morrison in 1968, Sia Furler singing "Destiny"—but overall, you guys, and your needs and problems, are not the first thing I think about when I get up in the morning. Don't feel bad or get insulted—no reason to get all butt-hurt here. Although you are not the closest thing to my mind, you're not the furthest, either. You're just one of the many things I've got to handle from day to day.

Being the Son of God, I'm needed in a hundred places at once, and it's impossible to hold on to a decent assistant. The cell never stops ringing, but when I try to answer, it always seems that I'm in a place with really awful reception. Plus, my dad's getting older—he's stubborn as can be, still wants to do everything himself. He shouldn't be driving at night anymore, but you can't tell him a thing; he's probably a lot like some of your fathers down there, calling to see how you're doing but also wondering if you might be able to tell him how to recover a deleted email or use "the Google."

With that said, when Chael asked me to write the foreword to his book, I couldn't say no. He's one of my favorite people; he's as sharp as a brand-new tack, funny, clever, and loyal. I stand behind whatever he says in this book, even when he contradicts himself completely and reverses his philosophical opinion over the course of five pages. I support whatever he says and the reasoning behind it, however elusive that may be to the normal, rational mind. After all, Chael has been a good friend and leaves me to my duties most of the time. And since it's a little difficult to find good workout partners during my travels, it's nice to know I can always drop in on him in Portland, throw on the ol' singlet, and get a good workout with someone who trains hard, isn't afraid to be honest with me, makes me laugh, and keeps my secrets. I love hanging out with him, and although he doesn't know it yet, there's a good chance that I'll be spending a lot more time with him in the very near future.

This is a really good book. I want to say the *best* book, but of course I can't put it before that *other* great text. (I truly hope you all know which one I'm referring to here.) Chael's manuscript is smart, funny, and most important, should help you make your own decisions and solve your own problems in my absence.

~~XXOO~~

(Chael, please edit out the hugs and kisses I gave at the end of my foreword. Realizing that some of your readers most likely won't be walking through the Pearly Gates, I don't feel it is an appropriate gesture. Oh, and make sure not to print this last part—Jesus.)

"I want to be just like Chael Sonnen."

That's what all of you reading this are really thinking, even if you don't yet have the self-awareness you'll have by the end of this book. I mean, let's be clear: you wouldn't pick up a book by Chael Sonnen and shadily park yourself in the café of your local bookstore (don't get me started on cafés in bookstores) to peruse the opening pages over your fat man's latte, let alone buy this book, if you weren't in some way interested in making your own thought patterns a little more like mine. Not that I blame you. I'm very pleased with the way I think.

What if you were given this book as a gift? That's simple. It means that someone very close to you wishes you were more like me, and that he or she found a perfect way to both give you a present *and* send you a message.

So, per your desire—or that of your loved one—this book will guide you through the most important steps to get you exactly what you want: to be more like me. This is no community college underwater-basket-weaving class, so don't kid yourself. The learning curve is steep, my thoughts are deep, and like any teacher-cum-celebrity author, I want you to come away from your journey as informed as possible so you don't end up embarrassing me later when you say, "Chael taught me that." So, before we really get going, I want you to go grab the following items:

1. A pen. To make *copious* notes and record your personal reflections when I blow your mind. No pencils. Do you see me printing my books in a medium that I can erase later? No. My word is permanent, and so should what you were thinking *contemporaneously* as you read my brilliant manifesto.

2. A dictionary. I use many big words that you will not know because our education system has failed you. You *love* watching people cockfight—and sometimes you even compound the joy by guzzling beer and scarfing down nachos that are all saucy trimmings and no nacho—so it's time to at least be honest with yourself that the little story you tell people about scoring in the ninetieth percentile on the verbal portion of your SATs is about as authentic as Donald Cerrone's little cowboy bit (more on that later).

3. A map. You will be following me around the world, and I am *not* there to take your hand and walk you to the nearest payphone if you get lost.

4. Your favorite photo of me to serve as a reminder of what you will become. No, the book jacket doesn't count. If you cut up, mangle, or even remove the book jacket from the book, I will consider that vandalism of my personal property. Now you've just offended the guy you want to be like. Self-hater. (If you bought the paperback and thus don't have a book jacket, I hope it's because you're a kid with a lousy allowance.)

5. A moderate amount of reasonably *healthy* snacks, like gorp (don't pretend you don't know that gorp is trail mix, you treehugger). I don't want you running away from the chance of a lifetime just because your stomach rumbles, and I don't want you to go crying to people later, saying that my book made you fat and useless. I am not, nor have I ever been, to blame for anything that might've made you drunk-dial your pals Ben and Jerry. What happens to you on your watch is your own fault. Stock up and strap in.

6. A *Tyrannosaurus rex* flying a fighter jet. I just want it for my own purposes, so render unto Sonnen that which is Sonnen's.

7. A beverage that will be suitable for drinking games. Yes, there will be drinking games. For example, every time I mention Brazil, you take a shot. You will be drinking a lot throughout the book.*

That's about all you'll need for now. I might remember something else over the course of this book as my brain uncoils, and if I do, run and get it but don't stop reading. It will teach you how to multitask. If you end up running into a pole or tripping on your plastic toy soldiers, you'll learn the hard way to be a multitasker. If you run into oncoming traffic, you're a couple of IQ points below a cactus, but you get points for dedication. So are you ready to go? Let's start turning you into me.

---

*No, I don't advocate the misuse of alcohol, you boozer. I didn't say that it had to be alcohol; I just said a suitable drink, meaning one that isn't going to interfere with your retention of highly valuable information. If you've recently woken up with a Sharpie-drawn Hitler mustache or *anything* fat and anonymous, chances are you'll want to reach for some iced tea. So don't go whining to the publisher that I forced you to drink until you threw up on your UFC action figures. And if you're under 18, read this book in the presence of a reasonably responsible adult. Consider this your disclaimer.

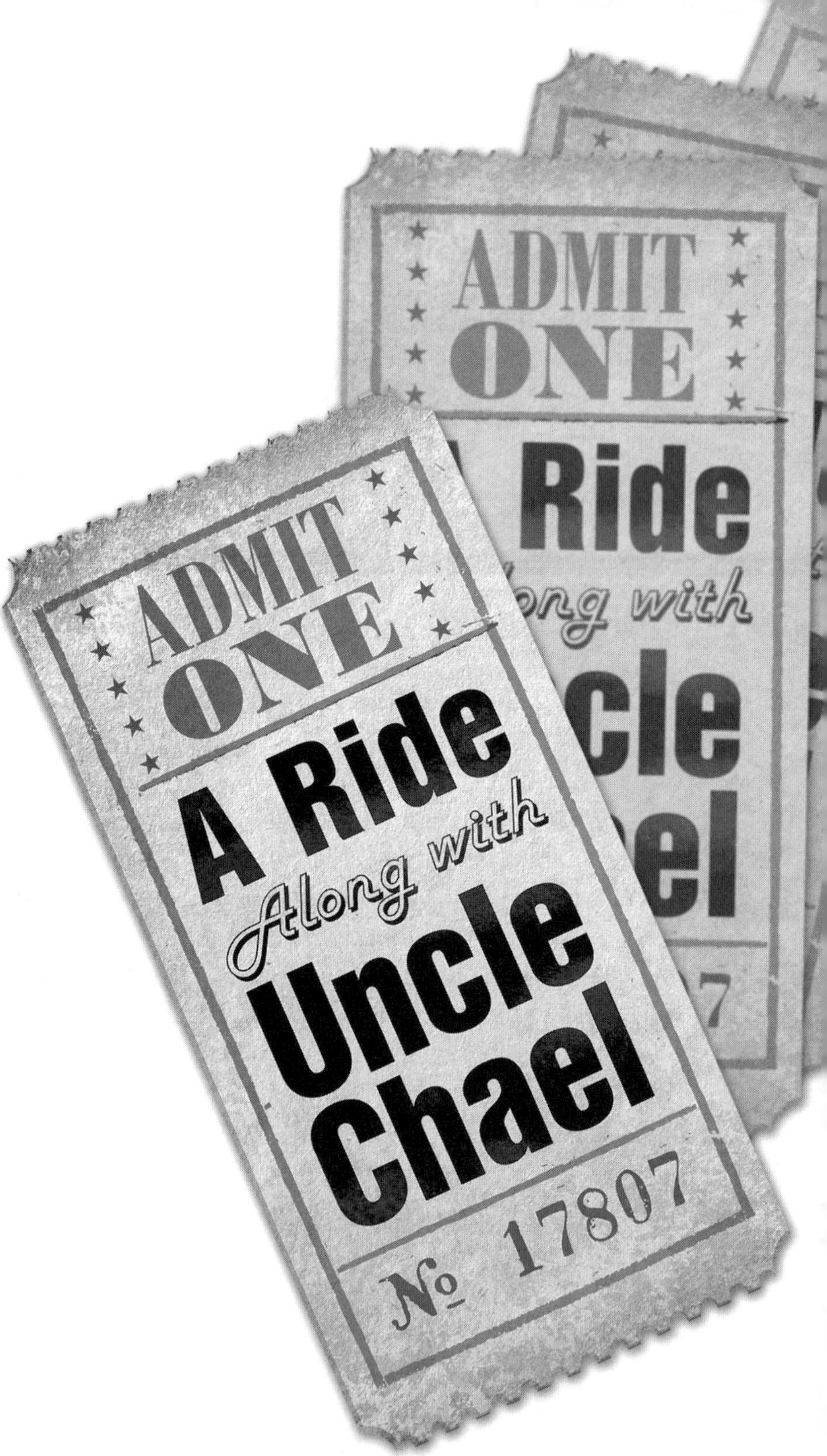
ADMIT ONE
A Ride
Along with
Uncle
Chael
№ 17807

★ know you can't see me, sitting there in your badly lit basement, surrounded by your five cats and a permanent odor that would cause anyone who dared descend into your living space to ask if you recently cooked broccoli, but I wanted to let you know that although I am about to take you on a journey through the professional MMA world, I am not wearing tour-guide attire, nor will I be holding your clammy hand. If you are wondering if I am qualified to be your Sherpa on this little voyage, I can most assuredly say that I am. I have been around this whole crazy ultimate fighting thing for a while now, and my involvement runs deeper than just being the man on the microphone or the Adonis-like warrior slaughtering his enemies in the cage.

Below is a list of some of the "other" jobs I've had in this wonderful sport:

★ Cornerman

★ Entourageur

★ Unwitting bagman

★ Uncompensated assistant

★ Exploited, well-intentioned doofus

★ Wearer of contracted T-shirts

★ Brandisher of sponsors' banners

★ Stacker of chairs

★ Deluded patsy

★ Keen-eyed observer

You see, I've played many roles in the sport, so I have some perspective. For your sake, I am not going to take you to an event where I stacked chairs.*

I'm going to take you to the big show, where yours truly is the man of the hour. I'm going to take you to one of my fights. You know, one of those events where I actually hit, get hit, hope to win, possibly lose. You packed? Got everything? Make sure—I don't want you knocking on my hotel room door the morning of the fight with a dry toothbrush or wet armpits, asking to bum some toothpaste or deodorant. I'm gonna be dealing with my own problems then.

So get in the truck. Sit in the back and leave me alone. Oh, and make sure to put on your seatbelt. The last thing I need is some trooper pulling me over on the way to the airport because you are bouncing around in the back like my five-year-old nephew.

TRAVEL

When I hear some windbag game-show contestant list "traveling" as one of his favorite things in his twelve-second mini-bio, I want to slap him because it is glaringly obvious he doesn't travel much. Traveling pretty much sucks in every fashion. But if you want to fight for a living, you've got to travel. A fellow UFC fighter isn't going to come to your hometown, barge through your front door, and start swinging while you're standing in the kitchen in your footie pajamas, enjoying

---

* Though I could write a manifesto on chair-stacking that would undoubtedly prove more beneficial than *The 48 Laws of Power; Rich Dad, Poor Dad;* or *The Art of War.* But the only people who read motivational, self-help, or instructional books are weak people (i.e., people who cannot figure out how to boil water on their own), and I refuse to believe that anyone insightful enough to follow Chael Sonnen (i.e., worship Chael Sonnen) needs coddling (i.e., breast-feeding).

a cup of hot cocoa. And Dana White certainly isn't going to hand you a big check afterward (unless you fellas have an "arrangement" that I don't want to know about). You have to go where the action is, and that's always somewhere other than home. So come on, we're already running late.

AIRPORT

"Long-term" (a.k.a. "cheap") parking is so far away from the terminal that I might as well walk to the airport from my house. So we troll the "short-term" (a.k.a. "expensive") lot, desperately looking for somewhere to ditch the truck. My cornermen, or "support team," are all with me. But being too cheap/lazy/entitled to drive themselves to the airport, they expect me to be their door-to-door limo driver, and I, a willing accomplice in my own destruction, have obliged them. I picked up one deadbeat in front of his trailer, another from his ex-wife's house (don't ask), and one at our gym. I'm starving, tired, late, and annoyed and can't find a parking spot.

There's one! Finally! Wait …

Compact Cars Only

Hmmmm. … While I am out of town getting beat up, is there any way the parking police will look at my dual-rear-axle crew-cab pickup truck and think to themselves, "I know it is not exactly a compact car, but it is compact compared to what Chael P. Sonnen *should* be driving, which is one of those bright yellow monster tractor-trucks you see crawling down the sides of diamond mines. I think we'll let it slide"?

It's a gamble, and the last thing I want is to come back to an empty parking space and a big towing bill to go along with my black eyes and split lip. I drive past the open space and then streak along, like a mindless comet hurtling to the outer reaches of the galaxy, my rearview an endless sea of compacts assembled in Asia. The terminal is now so far away, it is but a distant memory.

Finally we spot an open parking space—a garbage-strewn square lacking even the dignity of painted stripes—alongside an overflowing Dumpster. I park on top of Dixie cups, aluminum cans, and a small, white mound that is unquestionably a half-deteriorated diaper (or sumo attire ... No, we're in America, it's a diaper). My loyal companions and I get out and begin shambling toward the terminal. I can't help noticing that on the other side of a small fence, not more than five feet away, there are a bunch of empty spaces in the long-term lot, which we have now traveled far enough to reach and would have cost me thirty dollars less per day.

As we trudge along from a lot too far for even the airport shuttle bus to patrol, I balefully wonder what my guys managed to forget this time. Two hours before the fight will I see that desperate, glazed look in their eyes as it dawns on them that they've forgotten my mouthpiece? It's happened. I can see my mouthpiece now in my mind's eye—fifteen hundred dollars' worth of custom-made tooth protection that required numerous appointments and multiple fittings—sitting forlornly, neglected and forgotten, on the desk at our gym, next to some idiot's spit-cup of tobacco juice. That particular idiot, who forgot my mouthpiece the last time, is ambling next to me now, lost in his usual incognizant haze. I can only hope he's remembered my mouthpiece this time. The only thing I know for sure is that he's remembered to bring his supply of chewin' tobacco. I can see it, stored in his back pocket for easy access. He's also got a wad of it stuffed into his bottom lip. He's leaving a brown saliva trail as we walk (possibly useful for finding my truck when we fly back, but terribly disgusting). Although I may lose my teeth this weekend, I am comforted by the knowledge that soon enough he will most certainly lose his teeth as well, without anyone even having to hit him.

19

I might sound a tad harsh, but in the fight game, having a properly fitted mouthpiece is a big deal. When this small bit of protective gear was forgotten before, I watched my guys in mute horror as they marshaled their feeble mental faculties and bumbled around desperately, searching for a dodgy sporting-goods store. The end result? A five dollar boil-and-bite mouthpiece, like the one I had in Pop Warner Football, made out of cheap, hard plastic. A week-old orange rind would have fit in my mouth better, and it made me look like an amateur in his first Toughman fight. If there is a repeat of the missing-mouthpiece debacle this weekend, and I have to use another boil-and-bite, it will most likely fall out in the first round, and Joe Rogan, who misses nothing, will clown me about it to the vast PPV audience, which hangs on his every word. In addition, I will walk away from Saturday night with roasted gums.

There is one thing I am absolutely certain they have not forgotten: focus mitts. If I can't knock out a ninety-year-old narcoleptic with my Sunday-best sucker-punch, why am I going to warm up by punching mitts? Instead, I should warm up by practicing ducking underneath punches. Unlike me, my opponent can punch, and pretty damn well. I should focus on fine-tuning my specialty, which is grabbing guys, dumping them on their head, and then smothering them. So what's up with all the focus mitts? I have really begun to suspect that my guys (in fact, every fighter's "guys") bring focus mitts because they like walking around backstage wearing them. It gives them a sense of worth, a feeling of belonging. But if they are wearing them, they will undoubtedly be yelling at me to hit them. They'll shout out arcane numerical instructions, which are supposed to represent cryptic punching combinations known only by our little secret society of pugilistic initiates. My guys delusionally believe that these numbers will deceive my opponent, his entourage, or any intrigued backstage observer into believing:

1. I know any genuine punching
   combinations.

2. I am prepared to deliver them on
   command.

3. I have faith in my ability to punch.

I'd like to just level with these lummoxes and tell them that we're not fooling anybody. But my guys and their little bemitted hands need to feel like they have a purpose, a sense of mission. We've got about twenty pairs of focus mitts at our gym, in various sizes and various colors, and they've brought them *all*. They are stuffed in a bag bigger than the guy carrying it. I can imagine the fighters we've left behind, bereft in the absence of focus mitts, pathetically holding up rolls of toilet paper for each other to punch like a cargo cult with a rattan airplane— stubborn, delusional optimists awaiting our inevitable, triumphant return. While I am warming up Saturday night, if any of the talismanic status-confirming mitts should go missing/lost/stolen, there are myriad replacements on hand. There will be no desperate dash to a sporting-goods store to purchase new ones. They've made sure that there are mitts aplenty to hold for a guy who can't, and doesn't want to, punch *anything*. Punching things hurt. Damn, *typing* this hurts.

We finally reach the terminal. Slightly winded.

Check bags, then quickly off to join the interminable, annoying, re-dundant security cattle drive—shoes in the bin, all metal objects, blah, blah, blah. I head through first because I know that at least one of my guys will forget he's wearing a belt with a metal buckle, requiring its hasty, clumsy removal, followed by his ridiculous-looking attempt to hold up his baggy, rumpled pants, which will most assuredly fall down at one point to reveal his disgusting underwear.

I head through the ominous detector without sounding any alarms. A second later I hear a buzzer go off behind me and crane my neck. Just as expected, one of my guys is pushing his way backward through the now backed-up line of grumpy fellow travelers, removing his belt. He puts it in a bin by itself, where it rides alone through the X-ray machine like a kid on an otherwise empty special-needs school bus. I roll my eyes as he shuffles along, holding up his pants with one battered, gnarled hand. As he retrieves his belt and begins putting it on, I wait for his pants to fall down and display his retched underwear, but that never happens. I begin to think that maybe, just maybe, our luck on this little journey may be turning around. Then, just as I'm looking around for a vendor where I can grab a pop culture magazine for the flight, I hear the perfect Stepford-wife voice of the gate attendant over the airport's P.A system, cheerfully announcing the last boarding call for our flight.

As we begin to run, I wonder if the beltless genius has managed to buckle up. I also wonder how many focus mitts he decided to include in his carry-on, just in case.

PLANE

Sitting down. Time to relax and focus on the big day ahead of me? Not exactly. The bro sitting next to me has his darling little music-supplying device hanging around his neck, the headphones clamped to his ears, listening to tunes to "get into the zone." "What zone is that?" I wonder. And why he has to get into it, only he knows. It's not like *he's* fighting anyone. But there he is, maxing out the decibels so that everyone within the ten-seat blast-zone radius is assaulted by his cheezy metal music. He is cranking the tunes so loud that his head, which is huge and utterly empty, functions like a boombox speaker, amplifying and projecting one awful, interchangeable anthem of sonic misery after another into my already frazzled consciousness. I feel as if my collarbones are vibrating and my molars are about to crack.

I lean as far away from the source of torture as possible. Not only does this do wonders to stiffen my neck, but it also forces my head precariously into the aisle, so that it becomes an easy target for every oversized, stretched-out-pant-wearing mega-ass who thunders past. I chose the aisle seat in case I need to get up to stretch, or pace around, or go to the bathroom. But with the mini-monster-truck beverage cart, full of booze and snacks that I can't eat or drink, rumbling back and forth, and people getting up and down every two seconds to burp babies or reach above me to get only God knows what out of the overhead compartment, it's hard to find an opportunity to dive out into traffic. And even if I could, the line for the bathroom is longer than the two-dollar-bet line at the dog track. I see the bathroom in my mind's eye, and it is not pretty. Even though we just got on the plane, the blue-slimed, air-sucking commode will most likely have already been completely fouled by the tourists, crackpots, and frequent flyers who made it out of their seats, into the aisle, and into the bathroom before me. In my current state, I doubt I would make it through the door. Suffering from my weight-cut, my roiling, cramping guts would simply rebel at the stench, and I can't risk losing any more fluids. I already feel like a piece of beef jerky in the Sahara Desert.

So I sit. Heavy Metal Boy rocks on next to me, oblivious to all and everything except the flight attendants and the lukewarm beers they hand him one after another. He's guzzling bottom-shelf brews like he has a bushfire in his stomach. And the right cross to my chin is that I'm paying for that awful-smelling swill he's chugging. Yeah, Jim Morrison over here is one of my cornermen, and it's industry standard for fighters to pay for cornermen. I have a pretty good hunch which members of the industry conjured up *that* standard. The same guys who's Patton-esque mid-fight game plan is to "win this round because I'm not sure we won the last one."

Starving. Can't eat. Have to make weight. Nothing to look at except a little bag of peanuts on my fold-down tray. Right now it looks like a twenty-four-ounce, free-range rib eye. I take a sip from the little bottle of water the flight attendant gave me. It tastes like it came out of someone's pool. I have a headache.

An eternity of misery, and then the plane lands.

Time to get going. My guys have jammed their carry-on bags so tightly into the overhead compartments that we may need the Jaws of Life to remove them. I don't know for certain what is in those bags, but I see the very distinct shape of a focus mitt protruding from the side of one. Passengers behind us wait semi-patiently as my merry little entourage of cauliflower-eared miscreants take longer to dislodge their luggage than they would to dislocate an opponent's hip.

Finally, we're off the plane and headed toward baggage claim. I barely resist the urge to jump onto the moving luggage carousel, lie down, close my eyes, and allow myself to be loaded into the cargo hold of a plane going anywhere. But, no. I've got *work* to do. As we fight for standing room near the conveyer belt with the same people who beat me to the bathroom and made my life miserable during the flight, the bags full of stuff we really didn't need to bring chug past us. We chase them down and eventually snatch them up.

Outside, the UFC driver is already there, waiting. UFC drivers always are. They're like the Green Berets. I've never waited for a single one of them—and bless them, they've waited for me plenty ... and found lost luggage ... and been incredible problem-solvers and good friends over the years.

This time we have a fifteen-passenger van. There is a mad scramble for the front seat, which someone else gets, as usual. Other fighters, cornermen, and officials pack in. Collectively, the van is hauling more luggage than the Saudi royal family would bring on a monthlong assault of Everest. I get stuck in the last row, middle seat. The bags behind me are piled so high that they block the driver's rearview vision—

and protrude into the back of my skull, forcing my head into my chest. I spend the ride, which I'm hoping will be short, staring at my knees. My stiff neck is getting stiffer, and I'm pondering the imponderable.

HOTEL

The UFC pays for two hotel rooms—one for me, one for a cornerman. Fair enough. But I've got *three* cornermen. So as we're standing in line to check in, I pull out my credit card, knowing that a part of my fighter's purse for the weekend's grueling activities is already pre-spent on a room and a whopping room-service bill for my guys. None of them has a problem navigating the casino floor when looking for chicks or mischief, but not one among them can seem to find the twelve-dollar buffet. When it's time to eat, they simply pick up the phone in their room and order room service with the apocalyptic abandon of a sect of bulimic hermits. I don't want to sound cheap or downplay the importance of their job. After all, it is not easy to do what they do. How many people on the planet are truly capable of handing me some water, holding a bucket for me to spit in, telling me that the other guy "looks tired, we've got him now if you don't let him punch you in the face," or possibly carrying me out of the cage while making sure my neck doesn't suffer any more trauma? Ten? Fifteen? I don't know the exact number, but it can't be that many. I could always ask some fan sitting in the crowd to do what they do, but would he hold the spit bucket at the correct angle?

So I slap my credit card down on the counter, I order up the rooms, and off we go. Heavy Metal Boy, seventy-seven dollars' worth of airplane beer sloshing around in his belly, has deafened himself on the flight, and now he has no sense of his own vocal volume.

"How ya feeling, champ?" he bellows at me like a roadie at a Guns n' Roses concert. In the sound-refracting confines of the hotel elevator, his well-intentioned but concussively painful exhortations make my eardrums split like rice paper in a wind tunnel. I nod and smile, wishing I was wearing my idiot-canceling headphones. I give him a thumbs-up, but he keeps running off at the mouth. *Yeah, gonna go get 'em. Rock 'n' roll. Yeah. Show time. Stick and move.*

After enduring an eternity of my cornerman's high-decibel, low-intelligence mantras, the door opens at my floor and I'm out.

ROOM

Door locked and latched. Plastic "Do Not Disturb" sign decisively placed on the outer knob, although I know full well that it will not deter anyone—fighter, fan, or the inevitable voice chirping "House-keeping!" at any hour of the day or night. Which is why I've requested that there be only one key to my room. More keys = more trouble for Uncle Chael. One key means controlled access, which is good. But it also means that when (not "if") I lose the one and only key, I will have to go down to the desk and get another—an embarrassing, but all-too-familiar, ritual. It's not the best setup, but if I want any peace and privacy, which I do, it is the best setup I have devised.

I lie down, thinking about material for the press conference and interviews. A few years ago I decided to just speak my mind—to be as entertaining and engaging as possible. Sometimes it is great and fun, and other times people don't get it (or they get it and it pisses them off). However it is taken, it is too late to stop now. I've created a "climate of expectation," and now I dwell on it. Gotta think up some stuff. For my next fight, maybe I should hire a decent writer and lose a bad cornerman instead. Until then, I've got to *think*. What's funny or interesting or provides a unique viewpoint on this fight? I can't just give the ol' "I'm looking to test my skills in the Octagon" or "I've got a lot of respect for my opponent." Those are plain-vanilla Chump Fighter answers to the softball questions the MMA "journalists" lob at fighters like me. But I know for a fact that silly questions will be slung my way from now until fight time, and I've got to come up with some good responses. My material is one of the things that keeps me around—it's something the fans and media have come to expect and, I hope, enjoy a little. Being a one-man show, I have to force my dehydrated, sonically-pummeled, about-to-be-clobbered brain to deliver some witty quips and clever one-liners.

My cell phone is in a constant state of ringing, vibrating, and flashing. It does whatever it can do to pester me to death. "Friends" call to say "Hi!" and "Good luck!" (Translation: "Got any free tickets to the sold-out event?"). Sponsor's representative calls. Gotta answer that one. Yes, we got the T-shirts, and the hats, and the banner. (Truth be told, I have no idea if we have the T-shirts or the hats or the banner. We brought a lot of bags, and I know we have *a ton of focus mitts*, but when it comes to my mouthpiece and the sponsor's gear. ...) I make a mental note to double-check all these things on fight night, fully realizing that my mind will be in other places and that the mental note will go unchecked. I'm so distracted and strung out by fight time that my corner could put a Viking helmet from summer-stock opera on my head, slide a Tom of Finland T-shirt over my shoulders, and hold up a banner behind me that says "CHAEL SONNEN IS PERSONALLY RESPONSIBLE FOR THE AGONY OF CHRIST," and I wouldn't notice. But, "Yeah," I say to the sponsor, "we got 'em, bro, no worries." I make the extended-pinkie-and-thumb hang-loose sign to reassure this guy from a T-shirt company (who is on the phone and can't see me doing it) that we've got everything, and we're good to go. I'll be repping his company's stuff at the weigh-ins, press conference, and ring-walk. The whole thing.

Room's dark. So are my thoughts.

I go through my mental checklist of things that can go wrong, like a doomed pilot figuring out how he's going to crash. I'm hungry enough to eat the hotel carpet—and I've got a pretty good idea what's been on the hotel carpet.

I'm in a non-smoking room on a non-smoking floor in a completely non-smoking hotel. Yet, my neighbors in an adjoining room have decided, rather abstractly, to interpret the term "non-smoking" as "no *cigarette* smoking." I can hear them mumbling, stumbling, and coughing through the chintzy, quarter-inch-Sheetrock hotel wall. Living up to my low expectations of them, not a single one of the stoners had the courtesy to stuff a hotel towel under the door like Dylan did at the Delmonico Hotel when he turned on the Beatles. As a result, the nimbus cloud of pot smoke does not remain in their room. The acrid, THC-laden fog spills out into the hallway, and from there into every room on the floor, most namely mine.

So now *my* room smells like I'm holding a Cannabis Cup. If the reek of pot is this bad in my room, where there is no pot smoking going on, how can the pot-heads even see through the smoke in their room? It explains why I keep hearing strange crashing noises.

I get off the bed and open the windows to minimize my exposure to secondhand smoke. But open windows = draft, and weight cut = no body fat for insulation. I lie back down on the hard bed and begin shivering in the darkness like a penitent monk. I have a choice to make: I can either be cold or be stoned*. I can't turn in a postfight urine sample that smells like Ziggy Marley's guitar case, so nothing changes. I allow the frigid night air pouring into my luxurious, temperature-controlled hotel room to battle the eye-stinging reefer smoke coming in from the hallway. Weigh-in is tomorrow. Pretend to sleep. Can't eat. Wish I had been born Saudi Arabian rich, or Asian smart.

---

* As I wrote this last sentence, it just dawned on me that I could have called housekeeping and simply asked for more blankets. Yes, even Mr. P has moments of stupidity.

WEIGH-INS

The UFC runs a well-organized, well-paced, completely-packed-with-fans weigh-in, which consists of fourteen to sixteen parched palookas milling about distractedly, shoving up against one another, waiting impatiently to get weighed like cattle in a stockyard. After the scale comes a moment or two of making angry faces at one another for photographers. Although it can be fun to an extent, it's also a trifle silly, like a really catchy pop song. I'm just grateful it's never too heavy. (The next day is always heavy enough.) The good part of weigh-ins is that they offer a chance to catch up with old friends, troll for sponsors ($), repeat unsubstantiated rumors and irresponsible gossip, tell outright lies as if they were the Gospel truth with a concentration of people with itchy Twitter fingers, snipe at your opponent and his camp (which is always filled with the same similarly deranged, useless cornermen/retainers as mine is), and look forward to gorging on all the foods that you've avoided for six weeks.

The weigh-ins usually include one or two hometown heroes who are fighting on the undercard. They are added to the roster to give the event a touch of local "flava," and these bumpkins can be seen wandering around wide-eyed, which is very sweet and innocent. There they are, fighters among fighters, and I think that is great. Enjoy the feeling for a while, kids … then go get ready. Tomorrow you will fight someone who has done some fightin'. Thanks to Joe Silva, the UFC has some great matchmaking, and every once in a while one of the hometown heroes goes out there and beats a solid, established guy, and the prelim crowd, which has a high concentration of the hometown hero's family and friends, goes absolutely nuts. And that's great for him, and them, but this isn't my hometown. I'm hungry, tired, thirsty, and cranky. I just want to get the weigh-in over with.

Knowing that the scale is waiting for me, my increasingly annoying and swelling entourage and I navigate our way into the cramped elevator and head toward the lobby, seemingly stopping at every floor. Once in the lobby, we make haste for the arena—through the casino, past the banks of slot machines, gaming tables, and the buffet my room-service-stuffed louts can never seem to find, even though it's *RIGHT THERE!* I just want to get this done, and then this guy walks up with his kid.

The kid is ten, maybe twelve, years old, and he's wearing a shirt with my name on it. He's got a Sharpie marker clutched in one hand, and a poster in the other. And in that instant, I don't feel hungry or tired or thirsty or cranky anymore. I'm overwhelmed and humbled that the kid and his dad care. They start walking alongside me, and I feel strength and a sense of happiness that is hard to describe.

Immediately, I stop to talk with them, oblivious to how many cornermen or UFC functionaries are trying to hustle me along by telling me that I'm late. This kid is getting an autograph and a picture with me, and whatever else I can give him. And you know what? I walk away feeling like *I* got the better part of that deal. How can you not get overwhelmed by someone who came all that way to meet you, to wish you well, and yell your name as you take your lumps, win or lose? The scale can wait. *Take one more pic for safety, Dad. Now you get in the picture with your son and me; that's where you belong. Hand the camera to my cornerman—he'll take the picture. It's the only useful thing he'll do all weekend. Just give him a second to get his focus mitts off. There. Got it? Lemme see. OK, good. What, you're thanking me? No, thank you, sir, for letting me in the picture with you and your son. It's my honor and pleasure. You keep believing and I will keep fighting.*

INSIDE NOW

My name is called—here we go. I waltz out and quickly remove my sweats. I'm a jock, so that is what I wear. What I have always worn. Easy on, easy off. Over the years I've watched guys wrestle harder with their clothes and shoes at weigh-ins than they do with their opponent the next night in the Octagon. Some guys show up in what can only be described as costumes.

One particular fighter regularly comes out dressed like a cowboy. He's donning the whole OK Corral getup—garish "row-DAY-oh" shirt; tight, dark "gunfighter" vest; even tighter Wrangler jeans; a dinner-plate-size belt buckle (purchased, not won at an actual Rodeo, which is where genuine cowboys compete for such things); shiny, super-pointed cowboy boots that have never seen a stirrup; and, of course, to protect him from the blazing sun at an *indoor* weigh-in, a ridiculous, ten-gallon cowboy hat (black, of course, so we understand what type of badass he is).

The first time I saw him in that outfit, I wanted to give him some candy because I was positive it was his Halloween costume. It was startling, and more than a little embarrassing. Naturally, I assumed he had lost a bet, and having to appear in public dressed like a fool had been the wager. Sure it would be a one-time affair, I wanted to rib him by asking where his broomstick horse was, but I figured that after losing such a terrible bet he wouldn't be in the mood for humor. A few months later, my whole losing-a-bet theory was shattered when I saw him at other weigh-ins dressed in that same silly getup. I've since come to realize that it's his gimmick. I guess I also have a gimmick, which can best be described as the persona Pontificating Loudmouth. So, to be fair and honest, me and my gimmick are probably more annoying and distracting than him and his. Regardless, it is too late for either of us to stop now. He's got to keep dressing up like Bat Masterson, and I've got to keep talking a world of garbage whenever a microphone is shoved anywhere near my mouth.

All of us who fight for a living need to find a way to get ourselves out there. To each his own. Good luck tomorrow, Cowboy. Don't know whom you're fighting, and having to focus on my own circumstances, I won't find out how you did for a while. But good luck.

Just took off most of my clothes. Time to get on the scale, Chael. I notice that rhymes. Maybe that should be a new game on the Price is Right. The Chael Scale. Plinko's getting old. And yes, I am getting punchy from starvation and dehydration. Dizziness and minor hallucinations? You betcha. I move toward the scale. *Easy now, one foot at a time. Right, now left. There you go, big guy.* Did it. Watch as the commissioner moves the little brass weights back and forth. He looks puzzled by the scale's mysterious operational intricacies, much like I was when getting weighed in the doctor's office when I was seven. The weights finally even out, and as always, I come in right on the nose at 185 pounds. God is in heaven and all is right with the world. Flex the bones where my muscles used to be and mentally transport myself to the McDonald's in my mind.

Step (stagger) off scale. Head across the stage to have one more nose-to-nose stare down with my opponent for the cameras, the crowd, and the kids on the Internet. Raise my fists as high as my thirsty, atrophied muscles will allow. If I can't raise them higher than this tomorrow, it's going to be a short night. I'll wake up in the middle of the Octagon, horizontal, with a crowd around me. Don't want that. Need fuel. Last few pictures, backslap from Dana White, the boss. He's really buff now, and I'm really dizzy, so when his palm strikes my shoulder, I just about pitch forward and do a face-plant on the stage.

Then it's done, and my opponent and I are replaced by two other sucked-dry, cantankerous combatants who have waged their own battles with travel, entourages, starvation, dehydration, insomnia, anxiety, fear, and fear's meaner, older brother, panic. Any fighter who tells you he doesn't have to deal with each and every thing I just typed is a liar.

The lead-up to fights is hard, but after the weigh-ins a sense of calm comes over me. I feel that calm on the surface because I can finally EAT, and I feel it on a deeper, more philosophical level because matters are kind of out of my hands at that point. I've gotten on the scale. I've made a contract with my employers and fans that states I will show up the next day and let them lock the cage door behind me and another guy a lot like me, and we will thrash each other senseless for their pleasure. It's like letting gravity take over. There's no way out but *down*.

I've heard that many people who commit suicide seem strangely upbeat in the days leading up to the actual task of killing themselves, and having been a fighter for some time, I'm pretty certain it's because the decision has been made, the hard work's been done, and the pressure is off. The only thing left is that act. I can understand and appreciate that mind-set. After the weigh-ins there is nothing left to do but eat and defend myself—in that order. Those are very basic, primal directives, and when you know that those two things are all that is expected of you, it brings a kind of tranquility and focus.

The Mean Streets of West Linn, Oregon

sk any stripper why she made the horrible decision to start taking her clothes off for a living and ninety percent of the time she will tell you it's because she is trying to put herself through college. It doesn't matter if she is eighteen or fifty-three. (And yes, there are fifty-three-year-old strippers—and yes, I just threw up a little in my mouth.) If there were actually that many strippers receiving higher educations, the professional business world would be a lot more attractive. In reality, there are only a handful of reasons strippers do what they do, and none of them have to do with earning a degree in astronomy. The same is true for MMA fighters. Fighters are constantly going on and on about why they feel they were destined to become fighters. It's all rubbish. A guy chooses to climb into the cage for a living because he was either a) loved too much or not enough or, b) because he is an athlete who simply wants to keep doing what he loves.

I fall into the latter camp, which doesn't allow me to recount a grandiose tale of woe on the coming pages. I wasn't smuggled across the border in a backpack, nor did I spend the first nine years of my life in a closet. My story is rather bland, and I think that is a good thing. Personally, I don't think the general public has any more tears left to shed for fighters who had it rough on the mean streets of Malibu. Even if I did have such an upbringing, which I didn't, I wouldn't tell you about it in this book. Personally, I feel there are far more important matters to discuss. Matters that would probably make the United States a better place to live if we all gave them just a few moments of attention.

However, the one aspect I will share with you about my upbringing has to do with wrestling. And believe me, this has far more relevance to my current position as a fighter than does a story about how some haunting figure in my family used to beat me with a buggy whip every time I opened my mouth. I started wrestling for two reasons: because it was expected of me, and because there wasn't much else to do. And when I say there wasn't much else to do, I mean it. I grew up in West

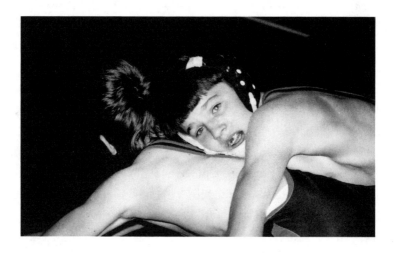

Linn, Oregon, which is pretty much the definition of "the boonies." My daily routine went like this: get up at the crack of dawn, do some chores, go to school, attend wrestling practice, come home and feed the animals, and then go to bed when the sun went down. We had a television, but it was black-and-white. No remote. And I didn't have neighbors, at least not any who weren't a long bike ride away, so except for the time I spent on the mat, there was zero interaction with other children.

I didn't have friends, but I didn't know that I didn't have friends. That's just the way things were. When I got to high school, I constantly heard people talking about crazy parties, and I thought they were nuts. The only type of party I knew about was the one where you showed up with your parents, gave some kid you barely knew a birthday present, ate some cake, and went home. Every time I heard someone mention a crazy party, I thought to myself, "I wonder whose birthday it was?" I had no idea that a group of my peers were going out into an abandoned field, lighting a huge bonfire, and plucking beers from a massive cooler.

Even if I had been invited to these parties, which I wasn't, I wouldn't have gone. My life was defined by wrestling. It's where I got my excitement. I happened to live in the nicest place in all of Oregon (seriously, West Linn wins awards for its pulchritude), but when it came time to wrestle, I was transported to Northeast Portland. At the time, Northeast Portland was nationally infamous because it was home to two of the most violent, notorious street gangs, the Crips and the Bloods.

Back in the day, Portland judges didn't just drop the hammer on criminals and send them to jail for life. If a judge looked across the courtroom at you and saw even a hint of goodness in your eyes, he would often give you an option. If you were an adult, he would give you the choice of going to prison or joining the military. If you were a juvenile, he gave you the choice of going to a detention center or reporting at five-thirty every afternoon to Coach Roy Pittman's wrestling practice.

As a result, I spent my youth wrestling with hardcore gangbangers. I was one of the few white kids in practice, but I never thought anything of it because it had been my life since the age of nine. The Crips wore blue and the Bloods wore red, but they were not allowed to wear their colors in the training room, so I never knew a rivalry existed between them. I never even knew any of them were in gangs because when you were on Coach Pittman's mats, you didn't get a drink of water or tie your shoes, let alone talk. At the end of practice, the Crips would leave through one door and the Bloods through another. I didn't even think anything might be amiss when I started routinely going to funerals. I had all sorts of teammates die, teammates who I looked up to, who were national champions and Olympians. I just thought it was all a part of growing up.

But for every boy we lost, ten more were saved, which is why I truly wish there were a lot more men like Coach Pittman around. The world would be a better place, and there would be a lot fewer kids in prison, or in the grave.

In addition to changing the lives of hundreds of youths, Coach Pittman was also a very interesting guy. Unlike most coaches, he had never wrestled in a single match. He didn't even own a singlet. Despite having never wrestled, he was the best darn coach on the planet. Why? Because he was a master motivator, and even more important, he was *consistent*. He never missed a practice, not once. And he expected us to be at practice every single day, including Christmas Eve. The only day he allowed off was Christmas Day.

I remember him showing up to practice one Friday night all dressed up. He arrived in his Corvette with a do-rag on and a beautiful woman in tow. He had asked Anthony Amado, who had placed fourth in the Olympics, to fill in for him so he could go on his date, but apparently he didn't fully trust Anthony and wanted to make sure practice got off to a good start. Just as Coach Pittman was about to leave, he saw something he didn't like. "I need *more*, Anthony," he shouted. Immediately Anthony changed the warm-up, but Coach must have found it still unsatisfactory because he flung off his do-rag, and the next thing you know, he's on the wrestling floor. His jacket comes off. Then he disappears for a moment and comes back dressed in his workout clothes. It doesn't take more than ten minutes before he is fully immersed in practice and his hot date is walking out the door. At the time, I couldn't believe it. It wasn't like Coach Pittman was leaving us high and dry—he had an Olympian overseeing practice, but he still couldn't step away from the team for even one night.

Coach Pittman's commitment to the team was insane. At one point, he was invited to go on *The Oprah Winfrey Show* to discuss how his wrestling program was changing the lives of kids who'd had a rough go, and he agreed to appear. But when he found out that he couldn't tape the show on a Saturday or Sunday, that he would have to show up at the studio during the week and miss wrestling practice, he canceled.

Yes, Coach Pittman gave up a chance to be on *Oprah* to ensure that we snotty kids got the attention he felt we deserved.

Another time after practice he held up two front-row center tickets to the Bulls–Trail Blazers game. The Bulls had Scotty Pippen and Michael Jordan then. With Nike's headquarters in Portland, the only place Jordan was more popular was Illinois. So Coach Pittman holds up these tickets and asks which one of us wanted to go. Every last one of us held up a hand. Then he said, "The game is on Friday night at seven, the same time we have practice. Who still wants to go?" Every one of us kept his hand raised. And you know what he did? He ripped those tickets to shreds and vehemently threw the scraps to the ground.

"Do you know why you won't go watch Michael Jordan?" he asked. No one said a word. "Because when you are competing on Saturday, he will be at practice. And that is exactly where you will be when he is performing on Friday." With that said, he made us all do twenty-five pushups.

Excuses did not exist in Coach Pittman's world, so he didn't allow them to exist in ours. There were days when we could hear gunshots outside, and there were days when the windows high above us would shatter, either from bullets or rocks. We never knew the cause because we weren't allowed to stop wrestling, not even for a moment. When sirens started howling outside, Coach Pittman would simply get up and lock the doors. He would say to us, "You can't lose focus, not even for half a second. If you suckas think half a second isn't a long time, then I want you to go home and turn on the burner on your stove. I want you wait until it is glowing hot, and then I want you to set your palm on that burner for a half a second. Then I want you to come back here and tell me half a second isn't a long time."

I can truly see the wisdom behind his words now. A half a second of lost focus can be an eternity, and it can also shatter a man's hopes and dreams. Need an example? Look no further than my fight with Anderson Silva.

There were many such lessons Coach Pittman taught us, but perhaps the most important one was that you take your responsibilities seriously. It's not about how you feel. There were dozens of times when the last thing I wanted to do was show up for practice, but I did because I had made a commitment. It's the same now. When I make a commitment to fight, I fight. It doesn't matter if I'm not feeling well or have a nagging injury. In the fight business, everyone feels sick before a bout and everyone has nagging injuries. That is why it upsets me so terribly when a fighter signs a contract to do battle on a certain night and calls in sick. And most of the time the reasons for backing out are pathetic. I've heard about guys calling in sick for staph infections. I've heard about guys calling in sick because they pulled their hamstring or hurt their hand. I have never missed a competition in my life because of illness or injury, and it's not because I haven't been hurt or haven't been sick. If you say you are going to be somewhere, you suck up whatever pain or misery you may be experiencing and you show up.

If it were up to me, I would write a forfeiture clause into the sport of MMA. Every other sport has it. If GSP signs a contract to defend his title on a certain day and at a certain time, he should have to do that. For Super Bowl 2013, the time and date of kickoff have already been set. Same for 2014, 2015, and 2016. If one of the teams that make it to the Super Bowl decides not to play because, say, the quarterback has a staph infection or a pulled hamstring or whatever the heck any of those excuses truly mean, a Super Bowl champion will still be crowned that day. The same thing should happen in MMA.

These are the types of things I learned growing up. I didn't have a tough life full of tough love, which doesn't make for an exciting story. But at least I'm not a prima-donna crybaby who covers my body in tattoos and thinks he has the right to call in sick. I didn't join the sport so I could cut in line at strip clubs. Fighting is an obligation, just like real life is an obligation. If someone were to kick in my front door right now, I couldn't say, "Geez, you're fifty pounds bigger than me, this isn't really fair." No, I'd get up off my ass and show him the way back out, which is what we should do with a lot of the current fighters.

So I just want to say, thank you, Coach Pittman for making me a real man.

Richard Nixon: Still My President —and Here's Why

Nixon was a *man*. Not a particularly handsome or well-spoken man like *yours truly*, but a true man who got the job done. Every documentary about the Vietnam era shows that same clip of Nixon getting out of a plane and flashing the peace sign with both hands, which is fine. But then immediately after this clip they always smash-cut to a montage of clips depicting various acts of 'Nam-era derring-do by our courageous soldiers. In these clips they are either dropping load after load of bombs or fearlessly patrolling the fetid Southeast Asian jungle with their M-16's (always with cigarettes dangling from their lips) or burning down "hootches" as "Charlie" flees in terror or on fire. They show clips of helicopters flying low, spitting death onto the enemy, the trees, the ground … well, onto just about anything and everything. Which is fine by me, but. …

Richard Milhous Nixon, patriot and president, didn't get us *into* the Vietnam War—he just did his best to *win* it. Nixon inherited Vietnam from … the Democrats.

Tell me, my fine friends and readers, have you ever seen a documentary or clip that associates either John F. Kennedy or Lyndon B. Johnson with the admittedly gruesome shenanigans in Southeast Asia? No, you probably haven't. Now ask yourself if that makes sense, knowing that both of those rogues had a lot more to do with it than Nixon. Wondering why that is? Let me tell you. It's because the people who make all those video montages are the direct philosophical descendants of the curs that brainwashed the country into thinking JFK and LBJ were good presidents and decent men. It's the same media men and women who ran the patriot Richard Nixon out of the highest office in the land, which he won in an overwhelming landslide—in a "mandate from the masses" unlike any seen before or since.

The media I am referring to is of the same lineage as the knucklehead reporters, writers, and journalists who provided the almost unspeakably pro-Obama coverage in this most recent, and most disastrous, "election" ("coronation by media" sadly being a much more accurate and descriptive phrase). This branch of the media hated Nixon. They hated him for his courage and his refusal to kiss their asses. They hated him for his work ethic, his moodiness, his love of true liberty, and his ability to get things done with grit, resolve, and determination. He was nothing like their shallow, pompous, glamorous, born-to-the-manor idol, John F. Kennedy. JFK had nothing on his own. The media co-manufactured his cheap, reflective pseudo-brilliance, and then they basked in it, like the reptiles they were and still are. And that is an important point—the members of the media *created* JFK so they could then associate with him. It was as good a way of picking up chicks on the left as ever there was. JFK and the media—a symbiotic, sex-crazed Frankenstein's monster, let loose on a gullible, trusting, and complacent country, which it then proceeded to pillage, both politically and psychologically.

46

If that last paragraph went over your heads, let me put it in simpler terms. The media invented JFK, then sold him to the voters, much like a recent political lightweight who was given the greatest push in the history of the American political system—Barack Obama.

But I don't want to veer too far off topic—this chapter is about an American hero. Nixon ran in '68 and started kicking some tail right off the bat, even as the media whined and cried about 'Nam (*They're shooting back! Run away!*). While the media expressed negative opinions about US involvement in Vietnam and the heroes who carried out the justified, dangerous missions, Nixon did his thing. The media didn't like that, not one bit, so they turned up the heat. They came at him and the American people with a well-organized blitzkrieg of bullshit. They basically instructed the American voters to elect his opponent, Hubert Humphrey, but the American people didn't buy it for one second. Nixon wiped the floor with him and became the leader of the free world.

So Nixon was put in the White House, where he belonged, and he got to *work*. He started droppin' bombs and letting the Russians and the Chinese know that communism had to go in Southeast Asia. He wasn't unreasonable. He was happy to sit, talk, and try to work it out. Not on *their* terms, but on *ours*. He was all over the place, in dark blue suits and a permanent five o'clock shadow. He was putting his finger in people's chests and telling 'em right where to go if they didn't like it, always backed by fellow badass Spiro Agnew, his right-hand man.

During this whole time, Nixon was talkin' zero trash, like a man; running a country in tough times, with a war going on and things to do. He was just doing his job, and then the next election rolled around. And guess what? The media, which hadn't been able to sit down in the last four years thanks to the licking they took while bent over Nixon's knee, decided to get some revenge. They doubled-down on the relentless, astonishingly biased reportage, basically demanding that the American voters elect Nixon's opponent, a pacifist, milquetoast, stumblebum named George McGovern. And I mean the shrillest, most overwhelmingly one-sided "journalism" in political history (until this last election, that is).

And guess what happened, my fine friends? Nixon won even bigger than the first time. The voters repudiated the media and their attacks both on Nixon the politician and Nixon the man; they gave him an overwhelming vote of confidence. The American people told the media, and their hollow, opaque, pandering coward of a candidate, "Thanks, but no thanks."

They understood Nixon and the complexities and demands of his mission, and they approved of what he stood for. How did they come to this decision? By *thinking for themselves*. They refused to be dictated to by a bunch of guys with microphones, news cameras, and notepads. The American voters *manned* (and *wo-manned*) up, and they sent Nixon right back to the hard work of winning a war and running a country, which was increasingly being undermined by the Left and its ideological shock troops, the media. The media, rife with individuals who had avoided the war by getting college deferments, had no interest in winning the war. Those war-avoiders had graduated from college with degrees in journalism and gone to work at newspapers and television stations across the country. Bitter and resentful, they bored their way into the supporting psychological structure of the country like a gang of shipworms, determined to destroy the timbers of the ss *United States*, even if that meant sinking the ship.

You see, those angry, defeated, invertebrates now held a grudge not only against Nixon, the leader of *their* country, but they also held an ever-growing grudge against the American people. They felt the American people had somehow wronged them by refusing to buy their line of bullshit in two straight landslide elections. The media could not collectively countenance the notion that the voters would reject the political hacks they, the media, had aligned themselves with philosophically. As the "unbiased journalists" schlepped back to their desks after the second landslide victory, a grudge burned and glowed in the hearts of each and every one of those cowards, and they waited for an opportunity to take their hateful, spiteful, cowardly vengeance.

Now Nixon ran with a bit of a rough crowd. He had a few guys around, the kind of guys you need every once in a while, particularly in the rough-'n'-ready world of the late '60s–early '70s politics. Knock-around guys, sure, but also guys with good hearts. Most of them had seen some action and done their share of work, clean and dirty. Personally, I wish I had a few of those guys around myself. They may have been able to give me some "advice" or "assistance" with some of my recent "challenges." Sadly, though, that type of associate, loyal and willing to break a few eggs for you if you tell him you want an omelet, is gone, long gone.

Anyway, a few of those fellas who hung around Nixon got involved in a bit of high jinks—nothing too bad. Nothing every other president's rapscallions hadn't done some version of, including the gangsters who hung around the two presidents that preceded Nixon—JFK and LBJ. Regardless of the commonality of their high jinks, they got into a bit of a jam. Nixon found out, and like a *man* he tried to bail out his guys. He did less than a perfect job of it. (Google Watergate—I don't have all day to give you people a history lesson.) The media, those flea-bitten, mangy, rabid dogs that had been skulking in the shadows, looking for a chance to strike, got wind of it. In the interest of the country, and the people, and the political system, they could have let it ride. But nooooo. …

With that white-hot hatred for the American voter still burning in their hearts, the media chose to destroy Nixon the president, the patriot, and the man. The media's prime mission was to punish the American voter for having the temerity to *not* be dictated to by them. Yes, my friends, that's the *real* reason the media grabbed ahold of Nixon at his one weak moment and refused to let go. In their hearts they had grown to hate America, and the American people, too much to just let it ride. They chose to sacrifice the American people's belief in, and support of, the political system for that one moment of vicious, crude, cruel vengeance. They made a conscious choice to make a big deal out of a very minor incident, knowing full well the damage it would cause. And, sadly, they succeeded. The American voter and the American political landscape have never been, nor will ever be again, the same. For their own perverse, twisted satisfaction, the media ruined a great man and damaged a nation's belief in its leaders for time immemorial.

And for what, I ask you? They sabotaged and hamstrung a military effort to battle communism by attacking the presidency, thereby forcing our courageous soldiers to fight a two-front war—the one against "Charlie" in the green hell of Vietnam, and the one against the greasy, cowardly, vile mongrels who spit on them on airplane runways when they came back to America. On their home turf, soldiers now had to deal with the brainwashed, slovenly, antiwar protesters. This behavior by protesters not only affected our heroes, it also affected our true enemy—"Charlie" in the jungles. It emboldened our enemy and allowed it to redouble its efforts to kill American soldiers. Eventually, it aided in our withdrawal from Vietnam, and we all know how things went after that. In the wake of America's exit from that part of the world, Pol Pot, a Communist mass-murderer in neighboring Cambodia, killed more than two million of his own people. Both North and South Vietnam fell into chaos.

Flash-forward to now. Vietnam is in business with the United States. China, too. And Russia. And everybody. They could have all had it back *then* if they had just done it Nixon's way and gone capitalist when we told 'em to. So just remember, the blood of every American solider who died in Vietnam is partly on the hands of every antiwar journalist and every hippie protester, and so is the blood of the American political system and the blood of President Richard Nixon. And let's not forgot that the corpse of the American people's trust in government is buried in their backyard.

Richard Nixon.

Still my president.

Rest in peace, great American.

It's Not About Left And Right
—It's About Respect

★ know all of you have been waiting for me, your New Champion of All Things Conservative, to start taking aim at President Obama. Although there are many verbal shots to take, there is something I'd like to share that will hopefully enlighten Obama Bashers and Obama Supporters alike. Regardless of my personal feelings, he is, first and foremost, President Obama. He was elected by the people of my country—the country I love, support, and would die for. He has chosen to take on one of the most difficult, time-consuming, stressful, and poorly paying jobs on earth. And personally, I believe his intentions are honorable and that he is doing his very best.

Out of respect for the man, and the office, I call him president. I do not agree with many of his policies; I am philosophically opposed to many of his political positions; and he and I hold radically divergent opinions on most topics. But as a man, and as an American, I feel it is incumbent upon me to support him, even if that means being a member of the "loyal opposition." My support may come in the form of silence. It may come in the form of respectful dissent. But it will be supportive, for the sake of my country.

I would like you readers to give that a moment of thought. Then, I would like you to compare my approach with that of President Obama's supporters in the years prior to, and even during, the election he won over John McCain.

Answer me this: Were they behaving as members of the "loyal opposition" when:

★ They were ridiculing, mocking, and belittling George W. Bush?

★ They used every means, fair and foul, to malign Bush, question his intelligence and decision-making capabilities, and describe not only him, but also his wife and children, in terms of contempt, cruelty, wickedness, and anger?

Why was it then (and still is now) that those on the left, the so-called progressives, always seem to fight the dirtiest? Why is liberal politics always the most cutthroat? Where was that type of personal, vicious attack on President Obama's character, his intelligence, his very worth as a person, from the Right during the campaign? It didn't exist.

For eight years the liberal Democrats put their own feelings, their own hatred, and their own viciousness in front of the needs of their country. Because they hated—absolutely hated—President George W. Bush. And yes, ladies and gentlemen, liberal politics is the policy of hate and aggrievement, first and foremost. Just listen to liberals speak. Watch their actions. You can literally hear and see the hatred leaching out of their bones, forming a poisonous cloud that infects everyone around them. Let me make a few things very clear:

★ Liberals don't love the poor; they hate the wealthy.

★ Liberals don't respect justice; they hate and seek to destroy anything they perceive as unjust.

★ Liberals don't even love their own ideas; they just hate everybody else's.

★ Liberals do not respect the rule, or even the intent, of law as a construct of civilization; they see it only as a weapon to dismantle their ideological opponents—to punish those with different ideas, different circumstances, different objectives.

★ Liberals hide behind the ever-shifting, amoral curtain of "social justice" to attack, destroy, and scatter the bones of industry, wealth, individual excellence, and personal achievement.

★ Liberals use the Darwinian concepts of natural selection and survival of the fittest (even though they are actually the ideas of Alfred Russel Wallace, one of his contemporaries) to force-feed the theory of evolution down every child's throat as a government-mandated absolute in public schools. Then they discard the notion completely when it comes to human beings who work harder, achieve more, and succeed in favor of a very hazy, nonscientific, constantly shifting notion of "equality" and "social justice," both codes for "hate," which they then use to strip from the fittest among us all the benefits of being fit. ("See that guy with the Porsche? He's better than all of you. Elect me so I can get rid of him, so we can all be the best together!")

Don't just take my word for it—listen to them *yourself*. Listen to how they always come out *against* something—some perceived injustice, some wrong *they* must make right. And while you're at it, watch how politically selective they are about it. Watch how they hold a press conference to denounce, ruin, and utterly destroy a broadcaster who inadvertently used a phrase or term that they perceive as "insensitive" to a particular race or ethnicity, all the while ignoring the fact that their lack of concern over that phrase for the past twenty years allowed it to slip back into the cultural mainstream through records produced by members of that particular race or ethnicity. Listen to how limousine liberals like Rosie O'Donnell rant about the fact that you are allowed to own a gun to protect your family, while she has *armed* bodyguards protecting her children. Listen to the hatred erupt from the bowels of her liberal guts as she hisses and screeches at everyone with differing opinions on same-sex marriage, gun control, or any other topic.

Is that how the conservatives act?

I have Democratic and liberal friends. In the eight years that President Bush was in office, eight of the most trying, painful years this great nation has been faced with—the attempted genocide of our people on 9/11, an international enemy with no face and no name trying to kill as many Americans as possible with no respect for humanity—I never once heard any of my enlightened, liberal friends refer to George W. Bush as "President Bush." I never even heard them call him *George* Bush.

It was always, without fail, simply the name Bush, spat out like a rotten grape. No respect for the man, his efforts, or the office itself. The same liberals who would lie on the carpet in the Oval Office to shine President Obama's shoes would intentionally spill red wine on it if President Bush were in office. But it's the *same carpet*, and the *same office*, and that's the difference I see in liberals and conservatives.

In assessing President Obama's job performance, liberals have been quick to deflect attention (and its subsequent and inevitable criticism) from some of the president's disastrous policies by sneering under their breath, "Well, he got Bin Laden." They do this as if all along they were hawks on the parapets of the nation, howling for the blood of that war criminal. They weren't. They were up on the parapets howling for blood, but it was the blood of a wealthy American or a conservative politician or a comedian who used an ethnic slur—not for the blood of the ideological architect of the mass murder of their fellow Americans. They steered clear of that, so afraid of "how the world perceives us" that they became declawed kittens lying on their bellies whenever anyone in the world raised the slightest stink about what we do to defend ourselves.

But once it was done, once that serial killer was sent to hell, where he belongs, the liberals used his justified death as a way to give President Obama a big "attaboy," while bypassing questions about his other atrocious policy decisions. And let's be real here for a minute. It's not like the president fast-roped out of a chopper with the SEALs team himself, with a knife in his teeth and a SIG P226 on his hip. And it's not even like it was his idea. (It *might* have been, had President Bush not already bravely instituted the policy of our nation as it applies to terrorists by saying, "We will bring you to justice, or we will bring justice to you.") But to be perfectly fair and honest, when the time came, when the question was put to President Obama about what do when Bin Laden's whereabouts were discovered, when the moral weight was on his shoulders and his shoulders alone, President Obama *did the right thing*.

Let me go on record here and say:

"President Obama: When they told you they had Bin Laden pegged, trapped in that filthy rat hole of a house, and they asked you to make a decision about what to do with him, you *stepped up*. You ordered the Navy SEALs to kill him. You did the right thing. You showed the courage, resolution, and conviction of the leader of the free world. I was *proud* of you, and proud to be an American with you as my president. I don't agree with many of the things you do or believe in, but you are my president and I want you to succeed for the sake of my country. I would prefer you to succeed and for me to be wrong for the sake of this nation. But I reserve the right to disagree with you, and feel safe, and comfortable, and free from the fear of reprisal should I publicly or privately support different candidates with different ideas in the future."

I love my country.

Greatness

When I was young I needed great people to help me realize my own potential. These people often came in the form of wrestling coaches. My first coach, Dave Sanville, did more than train me; he beat any shreds of indifference I might have had into submission. Don't forget that I coach wrestling on a daily basis, and I can say from personal experience that a lot of the kids who appear, to the untrained eye, to be mediocre actually have truckloads of talent. The reason they seem so average is that they don't care, and more to the point, they don't see a *reason* to care. The moment you give a kid a reason to give a darn, you have opened the door to his infinite potential. Dave went a step further; he opened the door, put up a welcome banner and gave me a set of keys, and then kicked me straight through the doorway before apathy could set in.

My college wrestling coaches, the great Ron Finley and Roy Pittman, built on that solid foundation and inspired me to know no limits.

Let me share a short anecdote about the sort of man who has the vision to shape a future generation into greatness. Awhile ago I was informed that Coach Finley was in the hospital, and his condition looked pretty grave. I dropped everything I was doing and drove hundreds of miles to his bedside. I brought him some cookies the size of Frisbees as a "don't die on me" incentive, and I walked into his room expecting to see my frail coach, mentor, and early adulthood hero for the last time.

I expected him to be a wreck, but Coach looked like Coach always did, aside from the silly hospital gown that showed more of him than I really cared to see. He also sounded like he always did. Between bites of the chocolate-chip supercookie, he reminisced about the training misery that he put us through, and he told me to go run two miles in twelve minutes on the hospital grounds because it was "easy."

A man in a hospital gown with a wrinkly butt and a potentially fatal condition was telling me to man up my training routine, and he meant it. I have a hard time thinking of a more inspiring moment than getting chewed out by a critical patient who could probably still wipe the floor with any healthy man. If you don't see the greatness in this, close this book and beat yourself in the face with it until you either lose consciousness or gain clarity.

Coach Finley made me the fighter I am today, and he taught me that if he can walk away from death just for fun, then I can do just about anything. I would not have been able to beat my most worthy opponent, Brian Stann, without his help. The first thing I did after that fight was call him at home and thank him for all his support and tough love. Do you want to know something crazy? On the phone he sounded healthier than I *ever* have. His "Well done, Mr. Sonnen" sounded like he was channeling the voice of the Almighty himself. That's a man, the sort of man I can only hope be. The type of man we should all strive to be.

More than showing me that I possessed greatness all along, my mentors gave me the tools to realize that I could achieve greatness on my own efforts. It's one thing to tell a kid something (and good luck making it stick), but it's another thing entirely to make that kid think he came up with the idea on his own. When a coach or teacher can convince a kid of his own authority, he is shaping greatness.*

---

* Or the world's next delusional militant dictator. It's a gamble, really, but remember, Adolf isn't just the name of a German Fascist. It's also the name of the guy who invented the contact lens, who was mentored by his uncle, *another* Adolf, who invented the tonometer (look it up). So, yeah, a little encouragement could lead to someone finding the cure for blindness.

My Latest Invention

■ f you keep up with cutting-edge concepts in science and technology, then you're probably familiar with particle accelerators. And if you keep up with my daily goings-on, then you probably also know that I am building a particle accelerator in my basement here in Oregon. For those of you unfamiliar with particle accelerators (also known as Supercolliders, or by the vulgate "atom smashers"—though we scientists tend to frown on that term), they are devises that fire atomic and subatomic particles at one another at super high speeds. The resultant collisions, and the particles they produce, are studied to gain insight into the very nature of matter and the origin of the universe. There are not many particle accelerators out there—the best one is over in Switzerland, but it's always booked—so I saw building one as a good business move and a chance to do some good science. You know, conduct some hands-on research of my own.

It's going OK, but it is a bit of a challenge, and there are some risks involved, including the possibility (remote, I believe) that I could accidentally create a black hole, which would then consume the earth, the sun, the planets, and a few adjoining galaxies. But so far, so good. Right now my particle accelerator is constructed out of some surgical tubing and an empty cereal box, but I've got some grant applications out there. If I can just get past the cutthroat peer-review process, I can get something published by early next year. Then maybe some more money will flow in and I can upgrade a bit.

So that's a work in progress.

I do, however, have one invention that is functioning absolutely perfectly, and has been for quite some time. It *never* fails, works flawlessly, requires no batteries, and is super low maintenance. It's a bullshit detector.

It goes off in my head whenever someone starts bullshitting. As a matter of fact, it went off this morning when I went downstairs in my comfy robe and slippers and put on the television.

I've been shying away from the TV news for a while now. Apparently, there is very little actual news. What has seemingly replaced the news is alarmist speculation. News used to be a guy sitting at a desk, telling us what happened that day, which allowed us to freely decide how to interpret that information. These days "news" begins with a few seconds of setup describing some dire, terrifying threat, including, but not limited to, terrorists, tyrants, melting icebergs, and chickens that give you a runny nose. This is then followed by *hours* of wild, apocalyptic speculation by nine or ten different "correspondents" and "experts" on the subject. Each weighs in on the terrifying potential scenarios, giving meaningless projections of future events that cannot accurately be predicted or influenced by a group of idiots in cheap suits in a TV news studio.

So now instead of one guy getting a paycheck for telling me what happened, there are ten guys telling me *their* versions of what happened, and all of them are getting paychecks. It's as if they get paid per word because each and every one of them slings bullshit as fast as possible, scaring me to death in the process. They tell me how to think, what to be afraid of, and whom to vote for.

As you can imagine, that's why I've been steering a bit clear of the "news" and trying to stick to nature-type stuff, hoping that it will kind of relax me a little bit. Ya know, shows about sea otters or dolphins or some such. But even those types of shows have turned against me. Let me give you a breakdown. About a third of each show is devoted to the furry or finned rapscallions gamboling about in their natural habitat. And then the hammer drops as the narrator or one of the researchers gravely intones:

"See this beautiful otter right here, the one you've been watching splash and dash gaily about for the last little while? Yeah, this one right here, cracking clamshells on her chest using a rock? Feeding her cute lil' otter babies? Swimming, diving, happy, and at peace? Well, by the time you watch this show, this otter, and her cute, furry lil' infant otter babies, will be DEAD. MURDERED. BY YOU … you selfish, heartless, miserable, fossil-fuel-consuming, global-warming-inducing, polluting pile of manure. This otter, yes, in fact this whole little otter family right here, died trapped in a nightmarish miasma of crude oil, battery acid, Styrofoam, and plastic that *you* created for your own miserable, cowardly, vicious needs."

What the narrator or researchers fail to mention is that while they might spend their time out among the otters of the world, they do so by avoiding adult responsibility and living on government research grants. As they point down from their moral high ground, they fail to mention that it is our hard work and taxes that supports them. Not only are they ungrateful; they are filled with hatred, anger, and spite for me and all of my hardworking kind. According to them and these shows, *I* killed that otter, *I* drowned that dolphin, and *I* am the reason that polar bear is staring forlornly at the shrinking ice floe, pondering his inevitable, imminent extinction. *I* have destroyed the world and everything in it, just so I could have a TV, a car, and air-conditioning.

So, yeah, even nature shows can get kind of stressful by the second commercial break, which is when they start to segue clumsily from a fun look at the lives of the animals into a political manifesto based on rubbish science, self-interest, and the scorched-earth assignment of guilt and its attendant condemnations. To keep my sanity, I flip the channel.

Oh, look, here's a documentary about the Old West. This could be interesting. About two seconds in, a modern-day Native American comes on-screen and solemnly pronounces:

"We lived in peace, until the white man came. ..."

And guess what happens then, boy and girls? If you're picturing a single tear slowly running down Uncle Chael's right cheek, you don't know me at all. What really happens is that my Bullshit Detector starts screeching like a depth-alarm on a torpedoed submarine hurtling to the bottom of the Marianas Trench.

Now, I know what you're going to say: Here's where Uncle Chael upsets a whooooole bunch of folks. And maybe I will, but I hope I won't. I hope you will hear me out before you pass judgment. Truly listen to what I am saying and give it some thought. Just remember, I'm not thinking any of this up myself. I'm simply relying on the wisdom and testimony of the great Native American thinkers who preceded me. They are my, well, kind of my spiritual ancestors.

So, first things first. *Nobody* lived in peace before *someone else* showed up. This goes for here, there, and anywhere. There is no historical or cultural precedent that indicates a continent-wide *Pax Americana* in this great country before Christopher Columbus "discovered" it—that the various Native American tribes and cultures happily coexisted. "Sources" make it sound like these tribes were jolly-good friends for centuries, hunting, fishing, praying, playing lacrosse, and participating in quilting-bees on the weekends, and then suddenly in the very late 1400s, this idyllic state of affairs was all rudely interrupted by the strangers with beards who showed up and introduced war, slavery, destruction, and genocide.

By the time Europeans arrived in the Americas, war, slavery, destruction, and genocide were already doing quite well there; they thrived just like they did in Europe, Asia, and virtually anywhere else humanity had ventured. Evidence shows that Native Americans practiced the exact same type of murder, slavery, torture, rape, cultural annihilation, forced starvation, mutilation, and general unspeakable mayhem on one another whenever the opportunity arose, just like every other culture did. There was no "line in the sand" that the Europeans somehow crossed, introducing inhumanity, brutality, and mass murder to an innocent, unspoiled, peace-loving hemisphere full of proto-hippies who wore beads and feathers and were satisfied to live in harmony and peace with one another. That's an Arcadian fantasy—a revisionist look back through a very distorted lens to a past that never, ever existed. When you put your brain to work, you realize that that lens has been intentionally distorted for the financial benefit of modern-day opportunists.

Not convinced? Here are a few things to consider.

The Aztecs and Incans (the ruling cultures in Mexico and Peru, respectively, at the time of European exploration and contact) both had gold. A *lot* of gold. Just *crazy* gold. Statues. Jewelry. Amulets. Entire hammered *sheets* of the stuff covering temple walls. It would be safe to say that they had a glut of gold. Moctezuma II, the Aztec ruler, and Athahualpa, his Incan counterpart, both had *buildings* full of stuff. How, and where, do you think they got it?

Let's turn this into a multiple-choice pop quiz:

a) As a reward for being a peaceful group of Indians, a proud and happy God made it rain from the heavens.

b) It was just lying on the ground in piles, like shiny anthills.

c) To paraphrase my mom when she deftly countered my frequent requests for money, candy, toys, or Pet Shop Boys vinyl albums for the millionth time, "Do you think it just grew on trees?"

d) It came in with the tide, and was then collected in whicker baskets by happy, singing, topless women.

e) None of the above.

You know the answer as well as I do, kids. This is how all that gold was obtained, broken down step-by-step:

1. Someone had to go out and find it.

2. Then someone had to go out and dig it out of the earth.

3. Then someone had to separate it from the dirt, rocks, and filth that encased it.

4. Then someone had to melt it down, refine it, and make it pure.

5. Finally, someone had to shape it into the phallic symbols South American Indians treasure so highly.

Not easy work. People generally don't volunteer to do it. They have to be … well … *forced* to do it. They have to be made aware that their options are limited to:

a) Provide the rulers with gold.

b) Die.

This is, interestingly enough, not altogether dissimilar from the options the Spaniards presented to those two sick serial killers, those two mass murderers, Moctezuma II and Athahualpa, when they showed up to Mexico and Peru. Granted, it doesn't make it *any more right*, but it was certainly *no more wrong* than what was already going on.

You don't have to take my word for this, kids. You don't even have to read the contemporary accounts of Prescott, Cortez, or Pizarro (the leaders of the Spanish expeditions of commerce, conversion, and cultural exchange in Mexico and Peru). You can go to Mexico and Peru and see *clear, incontrovertible evidence* of the gruesome goings-on pre-Spanish-contact, written and chiseled into stone in the *very hand* of the Native Americans who committed the atrocities. I warned you that traveling would be involved in this book, and now I am pulling that ace. Pack your bags, hop on a plane to one of these countries, and look at the walls on the temples still standing. Look at the paintings. You will see a clear, legitimate, cultural history of monoculture, monarchical inhumanity, mass murder, dismemberment, rape, infanticide, human sacrifice, cannibalism, slavery, extinction, and virtually every variety of human carnage and suffering that can possibly be imagined, and then enacted.

That's the pattern, the norm, the baseline. And there is no spike on the graph of niceness, friendship, collegiality, forgiveness, or peace. There is a constant, grinding, irredeemable horror that permeates the cultures of the Americas prior to European contact, and it winds its way through the centuries with a grim, immovable rigor.

How in God's name do you think Cortez or Pizarro, with fewer than two hundred men each, conquered empires with huge standing armies and populations in the millions? The men under Cortez's and Pizarro's command were not even professional soldiers. In fact, many of them had no military training at all. It's not like Ferdinand and Isabella sent the Best and Brightest, the Flowers of the Soldiery, fresh from the Moors, to handle the grumpy natives of the New World. So just how did they do it? Do you think they had flying suits like Tony Stark in *Iron Man*? They had some horses, yes. And they had some guns. But they did not have many of either, and certainly not enough to make even a slight dent in the empire of either the Aztecs of Incans. But they showed up, and within a few years they *took over*. How?

By having the support, endorsement, and gratitude of the millions of Native Americans whose cultures had been shattered and people murdered, mutilated, enslaved, tortured, and forced to pay astonishingly cruel tributes of goods, services, and human sacrifices by the Aztecs and Incans. When Cortez and Pizarro showed up, there was no shortage of Native Americans ready, willing, and able to throw in with the New Guys with the beards and bang-sticks since virtually *anything* was considered better than how they were already being treated. The unremitting horror of their existence under Aztec and Incan rule was argument enough for hope and change. They were eager to join the Spaniards and take up arms against their oppressors—who were from the same place, had a similar culture, and worshiped many of the same deities yet who slaughtered and destroyed them as quickly and brutally as they could. They joined the Spaniards as a form of cultural survival, a form of last-chance self-salvation, brought about by the most unimaginable conditions that had been imposed upon them by fellow Native Americans, not by "Whitey from Across the Water." Without the support of untold Native Americans, the Spanish expeditions would have been wiped out in weeks.

Think about this for a minute before you get all up in my grille and call me a bigot, a racist, or some other catchall epithet to divert attention from the indisputable historical evidence of domination, conquest, and inhumanity that was proudly left to history by its perpetrators, the Native Americans. It's not me saying this. I wasn't there. I didn't do it, and I didn't chisel the history of these actions into the walls of temples. But someone did, and he wasn't from Castile or Madrid or Lisbon or London. He was from … here.

> **Jorge Luis Borges wrote:**
>
> *Forget the onslaught/*
> *Of the bull that is a man whose strange*
> *and plural form haunts the tangle/*
> *Of the unending interwoven stone./*
> *He does not exist. In the black dusk/*
> *Hope not even for the savage beast./*

You don't need beasts or villains skulking into the harbor under the cover of night in a bunch of shipworm-ravaged, secondhand ships to cause a cultural holocaust. In this case, it was already in full swing by the time the Spaniards dropped their anchors, climbed off the boats with their rusty armor and primitive weapons, and started shovin' people around, looking for gold and makin' guys kiss a crucifix.

So. If you are Native American, and sulkily imagine yourself the latest link in a chain of victims that begins with the Spanish incursion, keep these things in mind: You may very well be the descendant of a slave *and* a slave owner; one of the oppressed *and* an oppressor; one of the mass murdered *and* a mass murderer. And at this point in time, it's just a little too far removed and way, way too complicated to continue to use the European contact and its subsequent cultural impacts as a platform to confer modern-day victimhood status and gain some type of advantage. The moment I hear, and people like me hear, the whole "We lived in peace 'til the White Man came" number, I kinda roll my eyes and reach for my wallet, wondering what it is going to cost me;

even though the white men that I descended from were from places like Germany and Scotland and had absolutely *nothing* to do with the Spanish contact. In fact, at that same time, my descendants were getting *their* asses kicked inside-out by whatever local, regional, or national Teutonic version of Moctezuma II or Athahualpa was running the show back then. They endured some pretty terrible tyranny, but I, unlike many others in modern society, am not allowed to claim victimhood based upon my ancestors' troubles. Am I complaining? Certainly not. I don't need some manufactured notion of historical aggrievement to succeed. Take it if you feel you need it. But let me share a solid fact: it's hard to pity and respect someone at the same time. Take your pick, and then live with the choice.

Social Media

Hey, are you friends with me on Facebook?

You know what, skip Facebook. Facebook sucks.

Social media lures people in by convincing them that it is essential for keeping in touch with their far-flung friends. People don't stay put the way they used to; we are go-getters and jet-setters who would feel nothing but shrieking loneliness if we couldn't touch base with our 564 friends and loved ones to remind us of who we really are. Whatever happened to making a good old-fashioned phone call, or writing a letter? I love letters. I even send them on occasion. I like hearing a friend's voice when he has exciting news, but I also like to be able to hang up the phone when he wants to ramble on about what he is having for lunch or what song he is listening to at that exact moment. I don't care, and neither does any other unneurotic human being. Social media doesn't facilitate friendship; it encourages using your friends for ceaseless validation. So, you had lunch? Anyone who gives you a "like" for that is fat (as in, "Holy catfish, Batman! I *LOVE* LUNCH! IN FACT, I'M ON MY THIRD!"). That person needs a gym membership.

Because of both hipster culture and Facebook culture, the human race is starting to resemble a school of hairy piranhas. Bad eye makeup and a few whiny albums used to be the coping mechanisms for the average teen with daddy issues. Now cryptic status updates, complete with the insta self-portrait, are the salve for their wounded egos. I have a violent allergy to self-photos. Get someone else to take your picture so that at least one other person personally witnesses your narcissism. What's that, all of your friends are on the glowing screen in your lap? I'm so surprised.

I especially hate the Facebook profile information. Most people seem to think that in order to come off as an interesting yet genuine human being, you have to be both open and enigmatic. This smattering of random facts resembles a drunk paint-gun rampage, producing a picture so blurry as to completely obliterate the outlines of anything remotely like a human being.

Don't believe me, do you? Fine. Here are some facts about me that I guarantee you didn't know.

★ I have hated mushrooms my whole life, but I'm beginning to change my mind about them.

★ I hate when I ask a question and it doesn't get answered.

★ I'm not into cars or trucks. Who cares? It's all Point A to Point B.

★ I miss Europe, but only because of the sandwiches. What's not to love about a place that puts a fried egg on top of every club sandwich?

★ If I could have one wish, anything at all, it would be for my dog, the Distinguished Gentleman of West Linn Mr. Danger Waffles, to talk.

★ I don't like snakes or people who do.

★ My favorite movie franchise is the *Bourne* trilogy with Matt Damon, and I think that the best actor to ever play James Bond is Pierce Brosnan. Not even Sean Connery brought James Bond to life like Brosnan did, and I don't care if you disagree with me.

★ I don't believe in UFOs, but there is a clear UFO phenomenon that I can't yet explain.

There. I bet you feel like you have known me since we were kids, right? You know everything that you need to know about me, don't you? Yeah, that's what I thought. You don't know squat, and you don't have a very clear picture of me, either.

See, these online profiles can be edited to be whatever you want them to be. Peasants on Facebook are worse, because by being the editor of their identity they have forgotten that they are trivial and anonymous and always will be. It's the same tactic crazy people use to appear lovable on dating Web sites, when they probably have some psychotic secret stashed in several pieces in their freezer. If they were so lovable, they wouldn't have to hide behind an online profile in the first place. Facebook fans, online stalker daters, same thing to me.

And why does "Facebook official" matter? I have heard reasonable, intelligent people say, "It isn't official until it's on Facebook." Is Facebook a legal entity that grants marriage licenses and religious ordinations now?

I have been focusing my criticism on Facebook, but it's not like Mark Zuckerberg is the only guy to blame here. Facebook at least allows for some semblance of dialogue. Twitter, on the other hand, lets every mouthpiece feel like he's addressing an adoring crowd. It shouldn't be called Twitter; it should be called Blather. No, you're not that important, and how dare you think you are. Nobody cares if you got tagged in that photo. None of us care that you're going to be at such and such a club on such and such a night. Twitter is moronic, and possibly the root of all things stupid and evil.

★ If you want to read more about my hatred for social media, check out my Twitter feed at @sonnench.

Why, Exactly, Are We Keeping the White Rhinos Around?

SLOW

ENDANGERED
SQUIRRELS

OK, eco-freakos, it's time to spar a lil' bit with that crude-oil-consumin', big-truck-drivin', air-conditioner-blastin', endangered-species-devourin' rogue, your ol' buddy ChaCha! Ready to trade some shots?

Before we get started, I have a few requests. First, go take a shower. You smell like a springbok that waded five miles through a swamp to escape a pack of hyenas. You don't use deodorant, so what did you expect? Next, take off the love beads, the hemp bracelet, and the organic-cotton dashiki. I know you think some barefoot Bushwoman from Namibia wearing mismatched American hand-me-downs decades out of style wove the dashiki while chewing on a mouthful of leaves, but it is actually a 50-50 poly-cotton knockoff that was made in a sweatshop in Vietnam right next to the fake *Twilight* T-shirts. I know, I know, you bought it at a street fair full of "fair trade" and "organic" merchandise, so it's gotta be real. After all, there are no hucksters in the world of green living, right? You've got a vaguely identifiable, hysterical need and no oversight, and that combo never breeds dishonesty or corruption, does it?

But wait a second. Didn't that fellow who sold you that "fair trade," "organic," hideous pseudo-serape look suspiciously like the guy manning the sausage 'n' peppers stand at last week's Italian-American street fair? You know, the booth you pointed at in righteous disgust before you turned up your snooty little vegan nose. They look awfully similar, that's all I'm sayin'.

Now I want you to remove those filthy Jesus sandals. God, if Jesus only knew that his name would become irretrievably linked with people like *you*, wearing shoes named after *him*, I think he would have fast-forwarded himself to modern times for a brief shopping interlude. Before heading back to the dust and distrust of the New Testament, he would have snagged his holy self a pair of Bally driving moccasins to gallivant around in.

Great, so glad you're out of them filthy, phony duds. Dang, you're a *scrawny* one, arentcha? Unka ChaCha is going to call up a meatball-parm air strike from my favorite pizza place while we getcha all scrubbed up. That's right, little guy, crawl under that translucent, shimmering column. It's what we call a "shower." Yes, that stuff coming down is heated, flowing water. It helps carry away dirt and grime. I'm hoping it can also carry away self-righteousness and stupidity, but that's probably expecting too much. There ya go! How's that water feel? You know, water has a friend, kind of a sidekick or lil' helper. He's like water's Tonto. We normal human beings call him soap. He's right here—I told him all about you, and he's dyin' to meetcha.

Now get under that hot water, grab that soap, and start scubbin'. While you're doing that, getting all warm and clean for the very first time, I'll go outside, chop down an endangered tree, and use its life— its very essence—to make a fire so I can burn your clothes, your shoes, your grubby accessories, your grimy hacky sack, that dime bag of skunk weed I found in your pants, and your well-thumbed copy of *Silent Spring*.

Finished? Good. You no longer smell like a plague-ridden rat. You still look like the lead singer from the Spin Doctors if he had been swept up by a tornado, spun around for three weeks, and then deposited in a cistern somewhere, but for you it's an improvement. Your cell phone? Oh, I burned that, too. Too many chemicals and minerals and slave-labor-manufactured parts. It hadda go. If you want to communicate with your girlfriend and let her know where y'are and what y'are doin', just bang out a coded rhythm on that hollow log like all those indigenous tribes you admire so much would do. Oh, she's in jail? Disturbing the peace again, you say? Well, I'm sure she did it for the "right" reasons. Throwing that brick through the plate-glass window of a Starbuck's during last week's rally against corporate America really sent a message to … well … somebody, I guess. Hope she's enjoying that orange jump suit and grape Kool-Aid in the slammer.

But let's focus on you, my newfound, newly clean(ish) friend. Here's a Team Quest T-shirt. Wait—gimme that back. Here's an Anderson "the Spider" Silva T-shirt for your emaciated lil' midriff. It'll give me something to aim for once we start our verbal sparring; you know, I hit him about 697 times when we fought. Plus, I've got *lots* of these T-shirts. Since he's got no fans, I scoop them up on eBay for two bucks a pop. I use them to wash my truck, which I do five times a week using as much clean, fresh water as possible. I like to make sure every inch of my "highway star" is gleaming, just in case I have to drive to a rally in support of Monsanto or Halliburton or Raytheon or any one of the dozen other evil corporate entities you battle like a mangy little Don Quixote; corporations that perform functions like creating drought- and plague-resistant strains of crops that keep millions of people around the world from starving, or technologies to prevent maniacs in turbans from frying your Mecca, San Francisco, with an atomic devise.

Washing my truck is a waste of water, you say? Well, exactly how is it being wasted? After it gets my truck all bright 'n' shiny, it goes down a storm drain, ready to perform another job. It doesn't disappear into thin air like Nicolas Cage's career or Kim Kardashian's dignity. It goes *back* to work; it evaporates, turns into a cloud, falls into rivers that drain into a reservoir, and gets pumped back into my pipes, so I can spray it on my truck and start the cycle all over again. It's called recycling! A perfect system. Aren't you proud of me, He with An Empty Head Who Points Filthy Fingers at Others? That's your new Native American name. Just thought it up. You like?

OK, enough of this shilly-shallyin', Nature Boy. It's time to start takin' some shots. Let's see what you're really made of underneath all that grubby unctuousness. Take this headgear and pull it over that empty head. Now put in this mouthpiece. God! When's the last time you let a dentist take a look at those choppers, Jungle Jim? What, no toothbrushes available at the sit-ins? Anyway, the bell is about to ring. Throw up your mitts and guard your grille. I'm about to spit some knowledge, and it's going to come hard and fast.

First things first. A little history lesson.

Your attitude and behavior are direct ideological descendants of the student-protest movement of the 1960s. It shares that movement's overwhelmingly self-mythologizing, self-referential, colossally reckless, insensitive, and vile aesthetic. Just so you know, the student protesters of the '60s weren't all students. They were a small group of semi-professional agitators who didn't fit into society and rode herd over a bunch of lost, dimwitted, self-impressed, highly impressionable, sub-adults ripe for indoctrination and processing. In theory, structure, and practice, the leaders of the protest movement marched in philosophical lockstep with that other world-weary, grizzled, pimp and failure Charles Manson. And let me ask you this—did your ideological predecessors ever stop to think about how the lives of the overwhelming majority of college students were disrupted and derailed thanks to their protests and attacks? Of course not. For the protesters, what *they* believed in, what *they* wanted to tell the world, was the only thing that had value to them.

Thousands upon thousands of students, many of whom may have opposed the Vietnam War themselves but chose to manifest that opposition by voting and maintaining society, were inconvenienced. They had their entire academic lives upset and defined by the actions of a scurrilous few who occupied buildings, disrupted classes, and made unlawful and ridiculous demands on society and the institutions of higher learning that they targeted. Hopped up on illegal drugs, they fomented showdown after showdown with the forces of reason, law, and order—with disastrous results. I often speculate on the actual nature of that famous photo taken at Kent State: a young hippie woman, looking, I should observe, not unlike Squeaky Fromme, kneeling down over the prone body of some male hippie, her mouth frozen in a scream, her agony captured for all time by a clever and fortunate fellow hippie photographer. I wonder if that young man lying there, instead of being the victim of some justified act of self-defense meted out by some heroic National Guardsman, isn't actually just laid out in the middle of the street in a narcotic haze from a bag of really potent dope. I also wonder if his aggrieved female counterpart isn't just screaming to their dealer across the way for another bag, so she can join him in the land of Nod for a while*.

That is *your* heritage, friend. That is whom you take your cues from.

Feelin' the heat yet, Activist Boy? Seems like it. You're starting to sweat a lil' bit. Starting to stink again, too. But this time you reek like a root cellar full of musty rutabagas. We gotta get some deodorant on you, stat.

To make some of my better points, let's head out on a safari. It's important. There are some rhinos that need our help!

That's right, save the rhinos ... or the pronghorn antelope, or the dung beetle, or the meerkat, or whatever your pathetic choice of animal to champion this week as a way of vaulting yourself into my conscious-ness without any legitimate accomplishment or quality of your own. But let's go with the rhinos for now. Big. Cute. Deadly. Got no real is-sues with them. But if their numbers are dwindling, and they are, isn't that nature's way of showing them the door, like nature does with every species eventually? Didn't nature put us here, too? Isn't the natural order of things for species to eventually go extinct? Doesn't the fossil record indicate that everything dies out sooner or later? How do you know that nature, and fate, and evolution didn't put us here to get rid of them, so something better and more productive might rise in their place? How do you know that keeping them around by artificial means isn't stifling the development of a baboon with two brains that might cure cancer in five hundred years? Who are you, eco-boy, to decide? Why do you, and not nature, get the deciding vote on what goes on the species scrap heap and what doesn't? I know. Rhinos are beautiful, they're intelligent, blah blah blah.

---

* I had a hard time deciding upon "land of Nod" and "Land of Nod." The former is dreamtime, per Robert Louis Stevenson's poem, and the latter is the place Cain ended up after killing his bro. Pick whichever meaning you want based upon your disdain for hippies.

Like the whales. We've gotta keep them around, too, because someday we're going to be able to communicate with them. This coming from the likes of you, who doesn't even communicate with the members of his own family residing two towns over, which speaks the same language. But we keep the whales around for the extremely unlikely reason that we might be able to "communicate" with them one day. As far as I'm concerned, I'd rather get rid of them if it affords the benefit not having to put up with the likes of you, even if that means that my great-great-great-great-great-grandson is never going to get an email from friggin' Shamu. And what is Shamu going to say, anyway? "Hey, humans. This is a chain email. Bring me some fish and a cute female whale to mate with. Then leave me alone or I'll bite ya in half."

Trees. Got to save the trees. Majestic giants, leafy wonders, your bark-covered blood brothers. Right. Gotta fight those evil lumberjacks. Don't let the fact that natural occurrences, like floods and lightning-ignited forest fires, kill more trees per year than human logging. Inconvenient truth, and leaves you nothing to scream about and no one to scream *at*. It's frustrating, I know, because how can you feel morally superior to a swollen river or an electrically charged thundercloud? Neither of them cares about you, and neither of them will throw fifty dollars of guilt money into a *paper* envelope and send it to your annoying tree charity of choice, just to make you shut up and go away. So that leaves *us* for you to annoy, and pester, and feel better than. As for me, I like the fact that trees exist so they can be cut down, and used to build things, like hospitals, and schools, and airports, and research labs. I like that. I want more of that. The older and bigger the tree that gets cut down, the better. It's had a wonderful, glorious, long life. It is getting closer (by dint of probability) to dying every second in a fire, or flood, or by disease, and getting rid of it will open a hole in the forest canopy that will let sunlight in, which will then help to make the area ready for a new tree, which would never have existed had that selfish old bastard of a tree, and an idiot accomplice like you, had their druthers. In fact, two or three trees might be able to grow, and thrive, in that old tree's place. So what are you saving it for? We need building materials. We need paper. What do you want to do, wipe your ass with an old cat?

And how old is old? How big is big? Where do you draw the line as far as which tree to protect and which goes into my next roll of double-quilted, extra-soft TP? How tall? Fifty Feet? Sixty? Eighty? And how old? A hundred years? A hundred and twenty-five? A hundred and fifty? What qualifies as salvation worthy? You'll sit there in the leaf litter, tearfully bemoaning this poor "elder" as the chain saws get fired up, as long as someone is paying attention to *you*. But you haven't sent your own grandmother a Christmas card in eleven years. You'll chain yourself to an old-growth redwood as long as a guy with a camera from CNN or the Discovery Channel shows up, but you won't volunteer at an old-age home or a homeless shelter.

See, it's not about the rhinos, or the whales, or the trees.

It's ...

about ...

you.

The constant in any radical ecological movement is not a concern for nature. It is a humongous, overarching narcissism. It is the belief in, and subsequent practice of, a form of enlightened fascism, a sense of entitlement, and a kind of conservationist noblesse oblige that dictates that attention be paid to *you*, and what *you* believe, and what *you* want. And, quite frankly, I don't care about you, or what you think should be done about any particular animal or plant. And raving at me about it, and making an ass out of yourself to get my attention or the attention of a very busy world, does not improve matters, and it does nothing for the species you claim to care for.

Stop crying, Jungle Boy. Some truths are hard to take. Sorry I roughed you up so bad, but somebody hadda do it.

Now pick yourself up off my driveway and go wash my truck.

For you aspiring MMA athletes who want to get into the sport to score chicks like mad, let me spare you some pain: most fighters are never recognized in public. Recognized as children left behind, maybe, but not in the way that will get you an adorably polite Asian giggling while she covers her mouth and flashes you a peace sign. From time to time, passing strangers even throw spare change into my teammates' coffee cups as they lean against a building looking like the homeless bums they could easily be.

If you want a job that will get you major fan recognition everywhere you go, do not become a fighter. Write that down. Now read what you just wrote: *do not become a fighter*. If you ignore my advice, your dream of being mobbed by beautiful women will not come true. In addition, you might as well tattoo "Don't Hire Me" on your forehead

because if you follow your half-baked ambition you will end up looking like a skydiver who packed a lunch instead of his parachute. Don't
believe me? Then listen to this.

C.B. Dollaway, an *Ultimate Fighter* alumnus and fellow decorated
Division I wrestler, went to a Kanye West after party (don't ask me
why). A gorgeous lady strutted up to his table. She was almost comi-
cally tall, blond, curvier than a racetrack, and—gosh, how do I say this
in a gentlemanly fashion?—rather robustly chested. She said to C.B.,
"Hey, has anyone ever told you that you look like Matt Damon?"

True, C.B. Dollaway does look like Matt Damon—like a Matt Damon who had the stuffing beat out of him, that is. I know it annoys C.B
when someone mentions it, but when the one who makes such a remark
is hot, the hotness dulls a lot of that annoyance. So he smiled and fished
for a compliment by saying, "Thanks, most people say that I look like
C.B. Dollaway."

You trolling bastard.

I officially love this girl, because she actually knew who C.B. Dollaway was and *she didn't recognize him.* In fact, she started making
jokes about how no one knew who the heck he was (even though his
season of *The Ultimate Fighter* had just aired). C.B. let her dig her
own grave for a while, and then he leaned in and shouted, "I *am* C.B.
Dollaway!"

Apparently (I wasn't there because I wouldn't be caught dead at a
Kanye West after party, let alone his concert), the color drained from
her face and then she left a girl-shaped cloud of dust as she hauled
her shapely ass out of the club. So, let this story be a lesson to you.
C.B. Dollaway is a decent fighter who had a good run on a television
show watched by literally millions, and even *he* isn't recognized by
hot girls. Imagine how mediocre fighters feel on a daily basis. Worse,
think about how *you* would feel. If you get into the sport for the love
of fighting, all the power to you. If you get into it for hot chicks, I hope
you will be OK dating Rosie and her five sisters.

BFFs

★ n many ways, my job is just like your job (unless you are a horse-reproductive specialist, in which case my job is nothing like your job; the only similarity being that we both wear gloves). To get ahead in my job, I compete against my coworkers. That championship belt isn't just a trophy. It's my corner office. My promotion. My Employee of the Month plaque. And once I have it, I'm chased down by all of those ambitious snots who think they can do better. But just because there is competition involved in the job doesn't mean I can't be friends with my coworkers. We can hang out, grab a bite to eat, talk about our days. And when promotion time comes around, we all fight to better our situations. My coworkers and I probably won't be best chums during the free-for-all, but once a winner is declared, we can resume our water-cooler gossip. This is a normal part of all work environments. This is healthy.

With that said, I have to mention just how much it irritates me when a fighter refuses to compete against someone because "he's my friend." Have you ever heard of a professional football or basketball player sitting out a game because a friend of his was on the opposite team? No.

Lyoto Machida and Anderson Silva are systematically ruining MMA by trying to make it into a diplomatic mission with four-ounce gloves. It's a *sport*, a *game*, amigos, and you two dancing macacos aren't princes with peace treaties. Did you ever notice that Anderson dips a toe into the light heavyweight division only here and there? Anderson chooses to hide by emaciating himself. Have you seen that guy on weigh-in night? He looks like a terminal patient, or the victim of some Dickensian illness—like Tiny Tim grew up and traded his crutchs for four-ounce gloves. I keep expecting that Santa Clause look-alike to walk into frame, take Joe Rogan's microphone, and start talking about how little it would cost to send Anderson to school. *For the price of one cup of coffee a day, you can make sure this Brazilian gets enough to eat*, and all that. Then you remember that what Anderson is doing is not only self-inflicted, but is just a means of avoiding being punched in the face by his best friend. I say that if you can't take a solid right from a person you trust, you have no right to fight a stranger.

In most sports, you expect to be on different teams during your lifetime, but in fighting your team is not your gym. Your team is your weight class. That means that we must expect to fight our own teammates over the course of our careers. That's the job, so if you sign up for it, deal with it. If you and your sister-for-life decide to throw a press conference to show off your best-friends-forever collage and your shiny new matching necklaces, maybe you need to rethink your career aspirations. Pinkie swears are bad for sports, kids. Swearing off competition against friends is just making athletes weaker, less entertaining, and less distinctive. I don't know—maybe Anderson isn't as hungry as he looks.

While Anderson is an easy target, there are plenty of fighters who are very quietly making these nonviolence pacts with one another. Why is this even tolerated in MMA? What are these fighters afraid of? I'll tell you: They're afraid of going up against the people who know their tricks better than anyone else. For the average fighter, it is scary to think of facing the person who has seen you train, who has experienced your strengths and weaknesses firsthand, and has seen exactly how their own training stacks up against yours. What's a fighter to do when he can't hide behind what his opponent doesn't know? You won't know what kind of person you are if you duck the people who are most likely to beat you. And you're certainly not a fighter.

very rock of wisdom added to the human race's collective hoard eventually gets another rock placed on top of it. As a result, the knowledge that we have now is better than what came before it. Jets are better than biplanes. Cars are better than horse-drawn carriages. Vaccinations are better than polio. Catch my drift? The people who get all crazy about the past—you know the types, the ones who go to Renaissance fairs in cloaks and tights, those crazy hipsters who run around dressed like the cast of *Mad Men*, and don't get me started about people who collect antiques—are delusional.

Do you yearn for the days when letters were handwritten? Do you wish you could go a few rounds with Hemingway (boxing or booze, take your pick)? Give me a break. Even Hemingway wishes he lived here and now.

Knowledge is acquired and honed, and when you really get down to brass tacks, it saves us a lot of time. Why make so many mistakes of our own when we can take this gift from father knowledge. Do we have to eat uranium and punch a lion and move to Brazil to know that they are all horrible ideas? People before us learned how to make bread, forge tools, tame animals, and get girls so we could just sit back and take advantage of the fruits of their trials and errors. What a wonderful world.

With all that in mind, when someone mentions the word "ancient," the first thought that crosses your mind should be, "Not as good." Sure, tradition can be nice and comforting, but at a certain point it holds us back from being better, smarter, more impressive versions of ourselves. Case in point: fighters who think they are part of some centuries-old martial legacy. I have a long list of grievances with anyone who fights just because he feels like he's an extension of some ancient order. I'm going to spare you my thoughts on religion for the moment, mostly because I just don't have the time to open that jar of pickled-pygmy-chimp fingers, but I'll just say that the wackos who treat martial arts like some sort of religion have, with a few very key exceptions to the rule, not achieved any level of enlightenment just because they can kick or punch a guy good. I hear that Steven Seagal is a holy man in some culture or another. Holy according to whom? Maybe the word for holy was confused with "I recognize you because the VHS of *Under Seige 2* is the only tape I have in this mosquito-plagued scab of jungle that I call home."

Most true athletes in the world, no matter the sport they play, will not act all pompous about the roots of their sport or claim to be more pious because they climbed a grassy knoll for some fresh air and a toke and found themselves in a meditation-cum-fighting salon with Bodhidharma and Musashi. True, most sports are pretty modern, but I don't see track-and-field stars mouthing off about their Greek forebears running around naked back in the day. You certainly don't see wrestlers embracing the roots of their sport by wearing togas and laurel-leaf wreaths around their heads, not to mention doing other stuff that spawned prison-time behavior.

So if the rest of the athletic world can stop with the high-handed speeches about their roots and the bratty behavior along with it, why do some fighters feel the need to swagger around and brag about being a member of an "elite, time-honored tradition." Fighting isn't about honor, and it sure as hell isn't about integrity. If we're talking about "the old days," as these rat bastards so often like to do, then what fighting really was about was either "you have something I want" and "I don't want to give you the something you want" or "I disagree with you, I am a king, and I have more disposable peasants than you do." Where is the honor and integrity in that? The only people who benefit from fighting are the fighters themselves, or the kings who get the spoils, making fighters the most selfish people on the planet and our job the most appalling in the universe. Anyone who pretends otherwise is not just selfish but unbelievably ignorant.

Look, any kind of fighting is brutal unless you throw in some dance moves and dress it up in pretty-colored sashes. Then you have Capoeira, which is about as effective as using lambs to stop a missile. Also, I am not keen on the term "martial arts." When I think of art, I think of Bob Ross—that guy on PBS who tried to teach you how to paint a tree—and a fat opera singer with a Viking helmet. Though to be fair, I bet Bob could've whipped the snot out of any strip-mall karate student while simultaneously dabbing some shrubbery next to those white porch steps because what person in his right mind would have a white porch with no shrubbery? It's ludicrous.

Just say "fighting," which is a science and a crude (but seriously fun and far more enjoyable) form of diplomacy. The people who get really insistent about calling it an "art" secretly want to be poets, and probably spent their lonely nights in bed writing haikus about clouds and leaves. News flash, Matsuo-san. Musashi became an artist only once he ran out of worthy opponents to whoop.

So martial arts are "time honored" and "ancient"? That's rich. It's a nice way of saying that something is dead and obsolete. If time-honored traditions were still so important to the modern world, we'd all still be taking trains and going crazy from syphilis. Stop pretending that you're tapping into some kind of ancient wisdom. Do you want honor and integrity? Go build a homeless shelter. Go keep a senior citizen company. DO something, because fighting sure as hell isn't doing anything. Look at Brian Stann: that guy fought a war, built a nonprofit organization, and can whip your ass, all while not being a jerk about it. That's a true fighter. In fact, Brian Stann has a distinction that only five or so fighters get to boast: he is a real fighter and a real man. What a rare combination, one that is never found in the same room as a *gi*. For those of you too busy talking about your roots, I suggest you take your pajamas, your rainbow sashes, and your dried herbal tonics to some stone monastery while the rest of us enjoy our penicillin, indoor plumbing, and the real fruits of ancient knowledge.

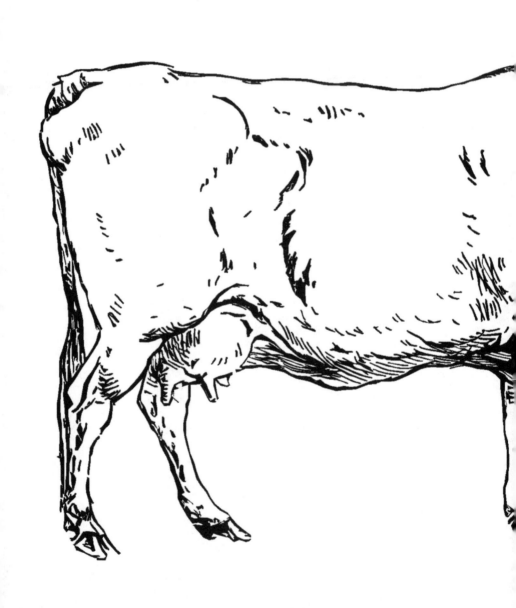

On Today's Menu:
Sacred Cow

Can't tell you how many discussions I've had with people, and how many articles I've read, about great films. The two films that are always discussed in a hushed, reverential tone are *The Godfather* and *The Godfather: Part II*. Let me make something clear: People discuss these films like they are brilliant works of art for much the same reason that people fall over when they get shot—because culture *instructs* them to.

Let's get the physics of the gunshot thing out of the way first. If you get shot, and the bullet has enough energy to knock you down, it should also knock down the person firing the gun. This is simple Newtonian physics and has been proved beyond doubt. Of course you have to take into account the instances when the bullet causes instant death, resulting in a lack of muscle control and inevitable collapse. You also need to account for instances when the individual being shot is off-balance or otherwise physically compromised from maintaining verticality, allowing the relatively mild nudge of a small lead projectile to affect his status. When such scenarios are removed from the equation, studies have shown that people fall down when they get shot because it seems like the right thing to do.

Why? Because films and television shows have instructed them that this is the correct and justified reaction. And so they fulfill their contract with their instructors by behaving accordingly. In most cases people function better, and stay vertical a lot longer, when they don't know that they've been shot. It happens in firefights and shootouts all the time. Just ask some of your cop or veteran friends.

Similarly, the culture of film critics and film buffs have anointed *The Godfather* movies (I and II)* with a status that far outstrips their genuine artistic value. They're not awful; there's some decent acting by Duvall and Cazale, but these performances are eclipsed by the unfathomable, self-reverential, slovenly, baffling performance by Brando, the usual bag-of-tricks mugging by De Niro, the stone-faced, self-impressed faux-portentousness/eye-rolling volcanic eruptions of Pacino, the high-school-play-level, off-the-wall antics of Caan, and the absolutely atrocious, mannered, stylized, vomit-inducing hamfest that is Lee Strasberg's "performance" as Hyman Roth. The movie is lit OK

---

* For the sake of legitimate academic and intellectual debate, I, the presenter of this argument, am charitably choosing to omit the existence of the third film in this series, for reasons that should be obvious to any and all interested parties, regardless of your critical stance.

in some scenes, but in others it appears to be working way too hard to brood. It's obvious that the director was trying to imbue the characters with weight and meaning by hiding them in the murkiness of poorly-lit rooms, hallways, and garages, but this attempt at "mood" fails, since the characters, a bunch of bumbling half-wits, don't have the weight of character to make themselves worthy of our respect, or their own dignity. As a result, their semi-concealment in the shadows does not lend them, or their actions, any gravitas. It simply makes it appear as though the mighty Corleone crime family has taken a bit of a downturn and had their electricity turned off by the power company.

I know. I can hear you howling already. I could keep this up all day, but instead I'll just point out a few things to think about:

1 **Why does a crime family of such might, weight, and ferocity send one old man (Luca Brasi) to a Mafia sitdown with no backup whatsoever?**
Granted, he was the most fearsome murder-machine the Corleone klutzes could cobble together to send into battle, but still, why was he there all by his lonesome? After he spends a few seconds trying to act tough, one guy stabs him in the hand with a knife while another strangles him to death with a piano cord. It takes all but twenty seconds to end his life. Seriously, I've had a harder time killing a squirrel in my attic.

2 **Why was Fredo assigned to protect the Don out in the street by himself, during a gang war no less?**
Who was giving out the assignments that day? "OK, we gotta protect the boss. Fredo, you're incompetent, an idiot, and a bumbling coward. You got this?"

3 Again with Fredo. We find out he somehow "betrayed" Michael, leading to an attempt on his life in the "fortified Corleone compound" by guys with machine guns. Later, Fredo says to Michael, "I swear, I didn't know it was gonna be a hit." So, when he let the guys onto the grounds carrying machine guns, what did he think they were there for, to play pinochle?

4 While Frank Pentangeli is being strangled, the guy robbing him of life says to him, "Michael Corleone says hello!" Number 1, what does that knowledge do for Frank Pentangeli in the afterlife? Number 2, it wasn't Michael who ordered the hit. So *why* lie to him as you kill him? Who is he going to complain to? The only answer, which one of my fellow movie pals came up with, is that he wasn't actually trying to kill him. According to my friend, it was a government plot to "turn" ol' Frankie Five Angels. But that's an awful lot of trouble to go to with a man of that age, with a piece of piano wire wrapped around his neck, to further some plot to make him a government witness, isn't it? Especially because you run the risk of killing him, and a bunch of other people, in the process. Whether it was a mob hit or a government plot, it makes no sense. It's a ridiculous scene, and it should have been ripped out of the script during the first read-through. Someone, anyone, should have asked the questions I just asked, made the same observations, and seen the wholly unsatisfactory nature of any of the plot outcomes. But this was obviously the best they could come up with for why Frankie turns into a cooperating, reluctant witness. With screaming and shooting and strangling and people getting run over by cars out in the street—just a colossal mess.

5 When Michael comes back and Hagen (Duvall) solemnly intones that Kay (Keaton) has "lost the baby," why does Michael ask, "Was it a boy?" Why does this matter? He already has a boy at this point (and a little girl, if my memory serves correct; I don't have the energy to rewatch this awful scene). What's the difference what sex the baby is? Or was it, as I suspect, just some awful way of wedging in yet another example of that eye-rolling, Lilliputian, mega-hack Pacino screaming at his fellow performers because he couldn't out act them? Duvall lets it ride; had Pacino tried this with a prime Gary Oldman, were they contemporaries, he'd have gotten eaten for lunch.

I could go on and on. If you want more, drop me a line after you read (translation: buy and read) this book, and I'll throw you a half-dozen more of this franchise's miserable bones to bury. The point I am trying to make is that I cannot comprehend how these films have achieved iconic status, which they clearly do not deserve. It's all part of the "cultural instruction program," which has also told us that *Precious* and *Philadelphia* were great films.

To counteract all this negativity, I would like to offer you ten films from roughly the same era as *The Godfather* movies, all of which are much better. Don't worry, I won't go all highbrow and mention some movie from Serbia that only nine people (including the director's parents) have seen. Some of these films you will have heard of and probably seen, but I am not talking about the chopped-up versions they show on TV. Before you get all "up in my grille" about them and start defending your precious *Godfather*, let's watch them together and then do a little compare and contrast. So go grab a tub of popcorn and curl up in the seat next to Uncle Chael.

THE MOVIES

Just for the record, we're not at the movies. We're at the cinema. That's what the French call it, and who am I to argue with Truffaut and Bazin? Pipe down, the move is starting. Wait, not just yet. I know we paid $13.50 per ticket, $6 for a coke, and $8 for popcorn, but we have apparently not been fleeced enough yet. We get the privilege of hearing a pitch for more Coke, a Visa card, and a pickup truck. Yep. Commercials in the movie theater. If you're an old-schooler like Chael P., then you remember the big come-on for cable TV back in the day. Twenty bucks a month and no commercials. Now my cable TV bill is $120 a month, and I get to watch that annoying gecko or those played-out cavemen or that hot, crazy hot, Flo from Progressive, whom I can just imagine stripping off that white jumpsuit and beehive wig so we can climb into the hot tub together and

Now that you know how Chael gets his groove on, let's get back to the movies. You ready for this?

CHINATOWN

Just an extraordinary piece of work. It's got everything you could ever want from a film: great acting (yes, before he paid more attention to his eyebrows and his front-row seats at Lakers games, Nicholson could really, really, act), great story, great sets, great lighting, etc. Just watch it. Oh, and the sequel, *The Two Jakes*, is pretty damned good too. Not as good as *Chinatown*, but better than the reviews it got. Nicholson's Jake Gittes, an idealist pretending to be a cynic, has so much more depth and character than anyone in any *Godfather* film. Watch him; watch a great actor, with a great part, create a great character, in a great story. Enjoy Nicholson's brilliance. It was all downhill for him after this.

THE EXORCIST

A horror film? Well, yes and no. A brilliant cinematic triumph, which used the story of demonic possession as a kind of palimpsest to write questions about faith, life, family, illness, fear, and mortality onto the culture itself. This movie's cultural and cinematic impact far overshadows that of *The Godfather*. So much so, it is actually embarrassing to mention them in the same sentence. Friedkin, the director, is a true genius. Seriously, if I were him, I wouldn't allow either Spielberg or Lucas to wash my car. He recreated cinema with this film. Watch it. Watch a master at work.

LAST TANGO IN PARIS

Yes, that blown-out boring wretch from *The Godfather*, Brando, was a fantastic actor when he didn't have contempt for the material and actually *tried*. Watch him in this movie, and then watch him as Don Corleone. He's laughing in his grave right now at the mockery he made of himself as Corleone. He actually appeared as Corleone (unbilled) a final time, in a film called *The Island of Dr. Moreau*. Rent it. You'll see what I mean. In both films he has the same contempt, the same self-congratulatory, breezy lack of concern or artistic integrity—a man fully at peace with his position above and beyond the material he has been given, comfortable, inoculated, warmly ensconced in the brutal, mercenary notion of his own private, smirk-ing, artistic joke. Then watch him in *Last Tango*. Watch the scene with him sitting next to his wife's casket. Listen to him, a great actor at the height of his powers, with a great script and a great director (Bertolucci).

LITTLE BIG MAN

A great film starring Dustin Hoffman, who would have made a much better Michael Corleone.

DIRTY HARRY

God, I love this film. This film sprang from the fertile ground of mid-'70s San Francisco and became an unintentional landmark of gay cinema. It held strong elements of the city's import to the national restructuring of cultural themes of sexual identity—macho pestering; the louche, lurid appeal of sexual slumming; the "rough trade" ethos. When Harry Callahan's antagonist, who is also Harry's gay "femme/bottom" alter ego, sees Harry's gun, he lasciviously intones, "My, that's a big one." This is mere seconds after Harry has spurned another anonymous potential male sexual partner in the rambles of Golden Gate Park in the middle of the night. That self-same antagonist, I should point out to you kids who aren't on board yet, is named Scorpio, an overt reference to Kenneth Anger's masterpiece film *Scorpio Rising*, commonly referred to as the Gayest Film Ever Made. Dirty Harry Callahan—an insane, inhibited, dangerously listing cargo vessel of repressed homosexuality, torpedoed below the waterline by his own unrequited urges, lurching ever closer to wrecking on the shoals of his own misunderstood masculinity—shoots what he can, beats what he can't, and ignores the opposite sex entirely. What a great cop movie, with such an interesting subtext.

A CLOCKWORK ORANGE

Insane, violent, visionary, original, challenging, brilliant.

THE GOOD, THE BAD, AND THE UGLY

Unjustly derided with the descriptive term "spaghetti western," this film stands as a great story, a powerful artistic statement, and a meditation on war, culture, religion, friendship, betrayal, and greed. It's also great fun and great entertainment, and it doesn't weigh itself down with ponderous notions of its own profound importance à la the two *Godfather* films I mentioned. When you rewatch this movie, I am sure you will agree that Eli Wallach would have made a much better Don Corleone than Brando, and that Lee Van Cleef would have made a better Hyman Roth than Lee Strasberg.

ALL THAT JAZZ

Almost criminally underappreciated artistically, Roy Scheider was an actor of the very first rank. As a performer, he was powerful, talented, versatile, and assured. Scheider never turned in bad work. He was amazing in *All That Jazz*, *Jaws*, and *Sorcerer*, a Friedkin remake of Clouzot's *Wages of Fear*. Without a doubt, Scheider would have made a better Sonny Corleone than James Caan.

VANISHING POINT

What a film. Check out Barry Newman in the white Dodge Challenger. Check out Cleavon Little as Super Soul. An existentialist essay on, well, I don't know. I'm not going to go all "film school" on you. Just watch and enjoy.

AGUIRRE: WRATH OF GOD

In this film, Klaus Kinski, a true and proper man and one of the greatest actors ever, plays a hunchbacked, mutinous conquistador on a doomed mission to find a city of gold in the rainforests of South America. Personally, I've had a lifelong fascination with Kinski. Back in '88 when I was just a young buck, I can recall my father bringing me to Studio 54 in New York to attend the book-release party for Kinski's autobiography, *All I Need Is Love*. I remember clutching my copy of the book to my chest, and brushing past Michael Musto and various other members of New York's nightlife royalty, and approaching the Dark Prince Himself—Yes, Kinski in all his demented glory, a shock of blond-white hair perched slightly askew on his huge head, his full, blood-red rubbery lips, and wide-set, incredibly blue and almost supernaturally piercing eyes, staring down at me momentarily as I stood there with a book and pen, hoping for an autograph. Only to have him sneer at me in utter contempt and turn his back on me. I still have the book, and I recommend it to all of you. Not the garbage, stripped-down, ruined *Kinski Uncut*, a reprint that was criminally "edited" (translation: destroyed). That book came out many years later to yawns and crickets, after Kinski had given up the ghost in the redwood forest of Lagunitas, California. I suggest the book despite being snubbed. I remember that my father took me to Chinatown to eat as a consolation for my failure to obtain the autograph—and we may or may not have gone to a restaurant whose name rhymes with "Ho Wop," and we may or may not have seen members of the New York arts-and-culture scene whose names rhymed with "Candy Marhol" or "Bavid Dowie," and we may or may not have snorted heroic lines of white powder that may or may not have been pulverized vitamins off the red-enamel tabletop in full view of the assembled patrons. But back to *Aguirre*—a great film and a great achievement. Watch, learn, enjoy. You're welcome.

So there is the list. As promised, all are better than *The Godfather* series. Again, *The Godfather* movies are not terrible, but they certainly don't deserve their status as great films any more than their mutant, stunted, bastard TV offspring *The Sopranos* deserved its years of praise as a great TV show. *The Sopranos* was, in fact, mediocre at its very best, and excruciating to the point of being unwatchable at its most mannerist. The acting was atrocious, from the top of the cast to the bottom. (Just look at how well they've all done since that lame horse of a show was taken out behind the barn and shot. The best any of them have done is a tequila commercial.) Yet this show was anointed as brilliant by the punditocracy at the *New York Times*. It was called groundbreaking, creative, original, and excellent. It was RUBBISH. But like *The Godfather* films, people were told it was good, and instructed to act as though it were a work of art. So if you want to do yourself a favor, and I know that you do, check out my list above. If you want to see good TV, watch *South Park*. There is more clever writing, social commentary, and character development in one twenty-two-minute episode of *South Park* than in a whole season of *The Sopranos*. My favorite *South Park* episode is called "Stanley's Cup." It's bitter, cynical, funny, brilliant. Enjoy.

Oh, right, the lesson … well … do your homework on the things you like and develop *your own* opinion about them. Don't be enamored with or disenchanted by critics unless you *know* the critic and relate to his perspective. Art is in the eyes of the beholder. Science, on the other hand, is in the eyes of the Lord—so if you get shot and fall down, unless the bullet severed an artery or exploded in your intestines, walk it off.

SACRED COW (2ND HELPING)

I know I've already touched on this Sacred Cow thing with *The Godfather* movies. But there is another culturally instituted, nonnegotiable concept that has got to go. This one deals with rock-and-roll guitarists.

It seems that we just all have to agree, by dint of the "ascended masters" of all things rock and roll, that Jimi Hendrix was the best without question, or review, or dissent.

And he *wasn't*.

Was he great? Sure. But he was also sloppy, his control of tone was less than perfect, and he died before he had a chance to register any significant artistic growth or create a massive enough oeuvre so as to enable us to do a comparative analysis with other great guitarists. Essentially, he fired a few shots that hit, and then hid in the weeds by dying. Make no mistake—he was a very, very good guitarist. But the Music Thought Police have declared him the Greatest, and anything other than slavish obedience to that notion constitutes heresy, which must be confronted, attacked, and burned at the stake.

Don't believe me? Try it for yourself. Bring up the subject with some music-fan friends. Mention the fact that you think Hendrix is a bit overrated, and that in your opinion there are a few guys who were just as good, and perhaps even a few who were better. Watch as they refuse to even consider your opinion, as they ridicule you, and as they question your ability to make such a pronouncement. Listen as they question your motives for making such a statement (including leveling charges of cultural bias and racism), and attack you personally. You may also notice, as I have, that the virulence of the attack is often directly proportional to the attacker's reputation and status (self-created and self-maintained) as a "liberal" and "free thinker." You will not be given a chance to bring up contrary evidence (say, by playing "Cowgirl in the Sand" by Neil Young). You will be ganged up on and shouted down by your friends. They will accuse you of ignorance, stupidity, and worse. Individuals like, I don't know, MMA Color Commentators, who fashion themselves as free-thinking libertarians, will become Lockstep Liberals who stand for freedom, justice, and diversity—*as long as you think like they do.*

Keep this in mind the next time you decide to enter into a conversation with your most "enlightened," "democratic," "liberal" friends about just how good anything—from something as silly, subjective, and meaningless as Hendrix was (or wasn't) to issues like global warming. You might see them a bit differently.

Don't say Uncle Chael didn't warn you.

Occupy
And The Turkey
Corollary

When I was in college, I studied sociology, which is a sophisticated way of saying I spent five years watching how
people become more idiotic as they band together.

I like to refer to this as the "turkey corollary": as a group grows larger and larger, the group's average IQ is only as high as the dumbest lump of nerves in the bunch. You could have a roomful of Nobel Prize winners, Mensa members, and ten flawless clones of me, but the moment a halfwit walks in, our collective powers are diminished by the bowl of brain pudding that is violently allergic to reason and common sense. Yes, stupidity *is* contagious.

A fine contemporary example of the turkey corollary at work is the Occupy movement. Don't get me wrong, I think people should be brave enough to speak up when they see injustice in the world. I just don't think they should follow the loudest voices (which are usually the dumbest) into some kind of pretend version of homelessness that disturbs honest people's lives. I am sure that there are some bright people somewhere among the Occupy activists, probably hidden by drum circles and the "concerned" parent dragging her five-year-old child into the opium tent for a "learning experience," but their critical thinking has been sucked into the black hole of embarrassing incompetence, hacky sacks, and acid trips dominating the movement.

The Occupy movement interests me on an intellectual level. Thousands of unhappy people who wanted something but couldn't quite articulate it banded together to create a big urban camping party and yelled, hoping that someone in the "one percent" would notice, read their minds, and then give them what they wanted in a gift-wrapped package without any political consequences whatsoever. Why did I ever run for office when there are so many much more brilliant analytical minds in the world? I'll tell you why, because I know that if I want the government to listen to me, I have to speak like an economist. I can't just, like, you know, man, I can't just *think* about how the world is, like, so messed up and stuff. I have to put my thoughts into a coherent message, approach the appropriate agency with my thoughts, and explain why my needs and the government's needs are compatible.

It has never been quite clear what the movement wants. Apparently, it's equality, but no one has offered any suggestions for how to accomplish that. People wanted their work to matter, so they quit actually going to work so they could park their butts in a public place. They wanted to create more jobs, and so they railed against companies that employed thousands of people. They wanted redistribution of wealth, but to no reasonable ends. Worst of all, they didn't bother to think through how they expected these demands to be met because they were more concerned with having other people get the job done for them. They wanted change, but a poem about a tree is not a credible voice, nor is an acoustic-guitar song about peace. Change needs to be quantified, calculated, and weighed against alternatives by people who are neither biased nor lazy.

Here is my point: The Occupy movement hasn't attracted brilliant people who have real ideas for change; it has attracted the worst elements of the human race to what has amounted to a high-minded excuse for a party. Mask an acid trip and a few sexual-assault cases with civic responsibility, and suddenly all the liberals are behind it. That makes about as much sense as leaving education policy in the hands of Playboy bunnies, who have clearly benefited enormously from learning how to read, write, and tally some numbers.

God help us, the turkey corollary is a more provable law than gravity.

For you kids out there whose idea of "playing a game" means sitting in front of a TV with a controller in your hand, blowing the heads off computer-generated zombies, this chapter title will have little meaning. Those of you a bit more seasoned in the ways of life and have actually played a board game will doubtlessly identify this phrase from the game Monopoly. The thought of this game will probably cast you back to picking up the card that carried this phrase, and from there it may cause you to recall the phrase that immediately preceded it. If you are still with me, then you might even have made the connection between that prior phrase and the desperate relevance it has had in my life. Yes, I just took a very long-winded and roundabout way to get you thinking about three simple, yet highly consequential, words—"Go to jail."

While working in real estate, the government charged me with money laundering, and I was completely guilty. Before you write me off as a degenerate, let me explain what the problem was. What in God's name does "money laundering" mean? If I were to come over to your house right now, knock on your front door, and ask you what that term means, would you be able to tell me? Moreover, would you be able to explain how to go about laundering some money? If your answer is yes to both of these questions, and you could show me detailed graphs to better explain the entire process, then you are either a lawyer or a degenerate. Personally, at the time I was charged with this diluted, mysterious offense, I was clueless that I was doing anything wrong.

Let me take you back in time. ...

I am twenty-seven years old and I just receive my shiny, brand-new real estate license. Having labored hard to earn it, I start to use it. I get a job and do what all real estate people do. I begin showing, pitching, hustling, selling. I've got clients and a boss and co-workers, just like everyone else. It's going OK. Getting a good, solid reputation. The schedule allows me time to train and coach the kids. When time allows for me to do only one, I coach the kids.

I'm heading mindlessly down this path, and then years later I receive a call. The voice on the other end of the phone is real friendly.

"Hey, Chael, I'm a big fan," the man says. "Love watching your fights."

"Great, how can I help you?"

"Well, I'm an agent for the government, and we need to clear a few things up. We need your ... expertise in understanding a few things."

"Sure, happy to help," I say. "But I'm no expert. I've only been doing this a few years—kinda learning as I go. Maybe talk to my boss or one of the good, experienced salespeople here? I'll put someone right on. Let me just put you on hold a sec. ..."

"No, Chael. You're the guy we think can help. Help us. Can you come down one day this week so we can talk?"

"Ummmm, sure. If there is anything I can do, of course. I'm your guy!"

So. Go downtown. Actually bring a few T-shirts to give to my "big fan." Even bring a few in smaller sizes for his kids. It's the least I can do. They're letting me *help* get rid of the *bad* guys. What I don't bring is the notion that I could have done something wrong *myself*. What I *don't* bring is a *lawyer*.

I get there and sit down. I'm expecting to leave in a half-hour, after supplying them with whatever meager insight my short tenure and low position in the office have afforded me. I'll leave a few T-shirts lighter and maybe with my very own plastic "Junior G-Man" badge.

Then the questions. They start innocently enough. General questions on broad enough real-estate-oriented topics—things I've told them I am no expert in. But then the inquiries begin to circle ominously back to the *third* deal I ever did, a deal based on the instructions and approval of my superiors. And I can't help noticing that my "big fan" and his fellow agents, who were slapping me on the back, laughing, and talking to me about my UFC fights just a few minutes ago, are now staring at me like a pack of hungry wolves staring at a baby bison with a clubfoot and a racking cough.

Why are they looking at me like that? I'm on the team, aren't I? I came down to *help*. I've done nothing wrong and have nothing to hide. But it's becoming clear—even to a well-meaning lummox like myself who stubbornly believes in everyone's benign and charitable nature despite a lifetime's worth of contrary evidence—that I have *no* fans in this room. In truth, I am a conviction waiting to happen.

My mind races. Should I have lawyered up like a villain in an episode of *Law and Order*? Are they going to slap the bracelets on me, read me my rights, and then lead me into the bowels of the building as if we were in an episode of *Dragnet*?

This *cannot* be happening. I'm a law-abiding citizen. A pillar of my community. I coach wrestling a few nights a week. The kids look up to me and ask for moral advice. I don't belong here.

But I am here, and the questions are getting more and more spe-cific. Copies of paperwork with my name on it—paperwork I ran past my bosses to make sure the deal was legal and ethical. *It's good, Chael. We do it all the time. Put it through.* I didn't even make any money on the deal. I did it to close out paperwork and move on. What the heck is going on?!

As I mentioned, I had no idea what money laundering was or how to go about it, so I asked my lawyer. This is how our conversation went:

Him: Think of the biggest library you've ever seen, and then mul-tiply that by three. That's the federal law library, and nobody, and I mean *nobody*, knows what is in *all* of those books. If you tell them that you didn't do this crime, and your statement has merit, they can simply dig into those books and come up with fifteen more charges to hit you with. They've chosen to bring you down. They've chosen to end your political career, and it's going to happen. Now, you can fight them and go before twelve people who weren't smart enough to get out of jury duty, or you can go along with them. Say you did it and go home.

Me: All that happened was one guy gave another guy some money. Nobody knew this law existed, including our team of attorneys who approved the deal?

Him: You are dealing with the United States federal government, the most powerful entity on planet Earth. Just hang your head and go home.

Again, I couldn't believe I had landed in that spot. But there I was, and there the charges were—hanging in front of me like a creature from the underworld sent back to destroy me.

And destroy me it did. It was a deal I barely understood. It involved a technicality I couldn't have identified even if I suspected it was illegal. I hadn't been around long enough, and wasn't a good enough salesman, much less crook, to conceive of it as an illicit moneymaking, or money laundering, enterprise. But that didn't change the fact that the deal and I are now handcuffed together like two brawling drunks in the back of a paddy wagon. There are no keys to this pair of cuffs. There is no way out or away from the whole mess. I am connected to this mistake for *life*. My political career, which I was hoping to begin full-time after I retired from MMA, is *shattered*. Any good I could do, any positive change I could have potentially made as a member of government, is *gone*.

Over a deal I didn't concoct. A deal I was told was legal. A deal I didn't profit from. And you people wonder why I act crazy sometimes?

The moral of the story is don't trust terms like, "We do it all the time." Even if you're just the grand fracking facilitator and not the scumbag proper, make someone else sign. If it looks like a duck, and walks like a duck, it's money laundering.

WALK THIS WAY, BUT NEVER TO THAT SONG

> "It seemed to me that his only sin was lack of imagination."
> —Jean-Paul Sartre, The Wall, 1939.

Sitting around the ol' homestead, engaging in some light reading of my least favorite French existentialist, I came across the above, which brought to mind something that has bothered me for a while—the uninspiring choices that fighters make in terms of their walkout music.

It's hard to believe that the vast majority of the poor lummoxes who fight for a living have atrocious musical taste and absolutely no sense of the power and drama that they could invoke with a good walk-out song, but unfortunately that is the absolute truth. Do we continue to allow them to molest one of our most prized senses in such a filthy fashion? Do we continue to stand idly by as they ruin one pay-per-view event after another?

Personally, I feel that those of us who have been blessed with a fine musical palette should help those who were clearly not. Whether it is seen by them as scolding for doing mankind a horrible injustice or as charity, this motley crew of offenders needs to be schooled in music much like a Brazilian plucked from the primitive streets of São Paulo needs to be taught how to use modern kitchen appliances like silverware. I've had it with the colossally unimaginative, puerile, sonic garbage that most fighters walk out to, and therefore the following is addressed as much to my fellow combatants as it is to you, my dear readers. I'm going to make some stylistic suggestions vis-à-vis walk-out music in the hope of improving the quality of events and thus all of our lives.

Let me start by making an official Chael P. Sonnen Rule. If you are a fighter, and so unoriginal and clueless that you come out with "Welcome to the Jungle" by Guns n' Roses, everyone in the audience is thereby allowed to throw one shoe in your general direction as that overrated, hackneyed, played-out trash-heap of a song heralds your schlepping decent toward the cage. If you clomp out to "Let the Bodies Hit the Floor" by Drowning Pool, everyone present is thereby allowed to throw *both* shoes at you. And if the ensuing deluge of hideous, over-priced, slave-labor-produced footwear does not pummel you to death or send you running back to your dressing room in fear of your miserable life, and you actually make it to the cage, you must wear a dunce cap while you take your beating. Harsh? I don't think so. How many times have you been subjected to those two crummy songs at fights?

Seriously guys, this is all you could come up with? Really? Both of those songs were bad enough the first time someone walked out to them, and it's not like they're getting better with repeated playing. If they sucked then and they suck now, it's safe to assume that they will suck forever. Forget that those songs ever existed.

Next, no death metal with Cookie Monster vocals. You know *exactly* what I am talking about. No one wants to hear a lead singer trying to mimic Lucifer in the pits of hell. (And by the way, why do we all assume the devil talks like that? How does he get anything done down there if no one can understand a word he says? Has anyone on earth actually *heard* him speak? For all we know, the devil sounds like Truman Capote.) If the embarrassing Cookie Monster vocals weren't bad enough, they are always backed up by dreadful, hyperspeed "music." So stop. Even if that's the garbage you waste your time listening to in the privacy of your own head, don't torture the fans with it. You have a *job* to do, and yes, a part of that job is to *perform* in the cage. But another part is to find music that tells a story. If that is too complicated for you, then let me present a more simplistic directive: Choose a walkout song that isn't sonically assaultive, incomprehensible, and annoying. In case that went over your thoroughly concussed head, let me spell it out in a way that could be understood even by those riding on the short bus: Death metal is *out*.

I also don't want to hear any country-bumpkin music. The arena you're fighting in isn't a honky-tonk, and you aren't in *Tayxus*. You fighters are all too young to have ever been in an actual honky-tonk, anyway. So enough with the awful country music. There's too much twangin'. There's too much steel-guitar playin'. And there are too many country hunks pourin' out their precious little hearts about the girl they lost or their home in the woods or the deer they shot or the job at the plant they lost ... or some other stupid, contrived story about living life up in "dem der hills."

Just so you know, every time you walk out to a bad country song
you are conjuring a single image in the minds of all those in the audience. That image is of a seventies country-music queen with a shel-
lacked mega-pompadour who is wearing a far-too-tight floral-patterned
polyester pantsuit garishly decorated with rhinestones. And when those
in attendance plug their ears in an attempt to block out your assault,
they hear that country-music queen in the back of their heads, wail-
ing and whimpering about how her *mayun* got released from the local
pokey and done run off with some other country strumpet who had
more teeth or higher hair. They know her song well because that's
what Uncle Hermes—the uncle who liked to give lots of uh oh-feeling
hugs—played when he'd take them up to the cabin for long weekends.
So while trying to block out your insipid choice of a walkout song, they
have to relive painful childhood memories.

Are you proud of this? It's not like you're keeping it real. Most
of these country songs are written and performed by people who no
longer live in the country, if they ever did (unless you consider Beverly
Hills or a penthouse apartment in New York the "country"). With that
said, I have to confess that I actually like country music, but I have no
illusions about it or its place in the sport—that place being *nowhere*. If
at this very moment you are thinking to yourself, "But Chael, you come
out to a country song," I want to inform you that I am simultaneously
thinking, "That's none of your damn business."

With country music out of the way, I want to address the whole
Mexican thing. OK, you're Mexican. God bless ya. I'm all for your
sense of cultural pride, but when some guy walks out to mariachi music, I feel like I'm having dinner in a bad Mexican restaurant. As you
begin your walk toward the cage, I always squint to see if one of your
cornermen is carrying a plate of sizzlin' fajitas (plate's hot, folks).
What makes it worse is that you don't actually listen to that music.
Your iPod is full of the same gangsta rap and up-tempo, modern music
as every other fighter's. You play mariachi music in your leisure time

and while training as often as you wear a sombrero to the airport. And why don't you wear a sombrero to the airport? Well, because it would look … *stupid*. All I ask is that you take that same rational mentality and cross-reference it with an image of yourself walking out to music that sounds like the "Casa Bonita" episode of *South Park*. I want you to really see and hear yourself, just as we hear and see you. If you do this exercise as I have instructed, a light bulb will most certainly flicker to life in your head and you'll stop with the mariachi music. I know this will leave you with nothing, but I've got some suggestions. If you want a song that speaks to your cultural pride as a Mexican, can be considered good music, and won't make the crowd smirk and giggle at your lackluster attempt to hammer home your inappropriate commentary on your cultural identity, try "Saint Behind the Glass" or "Will the Wolf Survive" by Los Lobos. Give those a listen. You're welcome.

The same goes for the whole Irish thing. You know what I'm talking about—the bad tin whistles; the screeching, bleating bagpipes; the self-conscious, single-minded lyrics and pathetic singing. Enough already. You're Irish. We *get* that the English raped your grandfather's sweet, sweet pride and that potato famine sucks. Can you play something as you make your appearance that isn't repulsive or make us uncomfortable with the self-dramatizing, self-pitying tone intended to remind everyone that the British heisted a third of your country? (I'm not taking sides on that one—at least not *yet*, not in this chapter.) Every culture has its gripes, and bad music that illuminates those gripes, but we're at a *fight* that we paid *money* to see. It's your job to get us hyped for the fight, not make us feel pity or guilt or indignation because your dear departed great-great-grandmama lost her "four green fields" to the Redcoats a hundred years ago, or however long ago that was. Most of you fighters boasting about your Irish heritage have never even *been* to Ireland, much less lived there. Under such circumstances, using the whole Irish Pride thing seems a trifle* silly, and more than a little lame and disingenuous.

---

*Oh, now you're mad that I used the word trifle. That too English for ya, Marcus?

Let me share a little secret with you: On fight night, as you walk to the cage, at that moment, we don't care about your self-appointed Gaelic-ness. Maybe tomorrow; maybe the next day; maybe never. That's our choice. So stop. If you absolutely cannot resist the temptation to try stealing a little of the romanticism of the "old country," at least make it upbeat and listenable. Deal? Again, I am not going to leave you high and dry, my dear sons of the old with sod between your ears. Try something from *The Snake* album by Shane MacGowan and the Popes. I will even tolerate "Going Back to Boston" by the Drop Kick Murphys. Forrest comes out to that; didn't help much when I beat him via triangle choke*

Moving on to gangsta rap. Again, I am going to share a truth known by apparently everyone but you. You are not a gangsta. Neither is the guy who made the music you are walking out to. He either owns a mansion somewhere in the hills or a triplex in a doorman building. Truthfully, he probably owns both. He also has an army of servants, which includes at least one personal manicurist. It has been well over a decade since there has been any interest in, or cultural cachet attached to, gangsta rap. You missed the boat, stupid. Remove all that crap from your iPad and stop living in a fantasy world. You aren't fooling anyone. We know you are not hopping in your "six-fo'" and doing drive-bys postfight. It's ludicrous. Enough.

Now, before I get to my lists of good and great walkout songs, I feel I need to get slightly more specific, just in case you have been brainwashed by popular culture into believing a bad song or bad band is actually a good song or good band simply because you have been told it is good a thousand times. For example, groups like Buckcherry, Wolfmother, and The Darkness will always suck, no matter how hard they are pushed by an A&R imbecile. I would go deeper into why and

---

*That is exactly how that fight ended, and I don't care what you saw on YouTube.

how they suck, but there are two other terrible bands that need much more attention.

Stay Away from
These Two Bands

Aerosmith and Metallica—the two biggest frauds in popular rock music. Let me start with Aerosmith, one of the great puzzles of modern culture. They were dreadful in the 1970s—their main claim to fame was a singer who put scarves on his mike stand. He just couldn't, well, *sing*. The guitarist is equally atrocious. He has spent forty years making a living from the first thirty seconds of "Walk This Way," which is, when you actually listen to it, just really, really mediocre. No innovation, no artistry, nothing.

Thankfully, Aerosmith disappeared in the '80s, but for some unfathomable reason someone at MTV decided they were "cool." (I still wonder if it was just a programmer's sick, twisted prank that got out of control.) They flung Aerosmith at the MTV generation like a rabid zoo chimp flinging a handful of excrement through the bars of its cage at an unsuspecting eight-year-old child; sadly, most of it stuck. Then, the band decided to do a duet with Run-DMC, to show how rock and rap had come together—a cynical, obvious, boring exercise in crossmarketing shenanigans. Rock and rap were *already* together, decades before this; go find, and listen to, "Hot Rod Lincoln" by Johnny Bond.

Aerosmith was awful, is awful, and always will be awful. They just relentlessly tell the world how good they are. No Aerosmith, ever.

Now let me dissect Metallica. They were an awful thrash-band from San Francisco or thereabouts going nowhere until someone at a record company began paying "special attention" to them for reasons that are best left ... undiscussed. They have metastasized over the years into a bloated, stupid, annoying bunch of balding, bloated boobs. But every metal magazine puts them on every cover for some unknown (or should I say "undiscussed"?) reason. And on every cover they're wearing their stupid rock-and-roll sunglasses on their "heavy-metal mean-mug" faces. They are rewarded each time they churn out a crappy, derivative record—which thankfully happens only every few years. Their singer spent a fortune on singing lessons that obviously didn't take, but that doesn't stop him from trying to "scoop" notes on every phrase, causing him to sound like a drunken businessman doing karaoke to Christina Aguilera at her worst. Metallica can be summed up like this: self-mythologizing, self-impressed, relentless, awful, with the most annoying, mullet-sporting "fans" of any band.

God, I wish Aerosmith and Metallica would do a tour together and end up with a suicidal airplane pilot. So *no* Aerosmith or Metallica, ever. No exceptions.

"What then, Chael?" you may very well be asking. How canst thou lead us out of our creative musical wilderness and into the sonic Promised Land, like a latter-day Moses? I can, my children; and will. Read on.

What Is the Role of Good Walkout Music?

At this point, I feel I have done a decent job describing a *bad* walkout song. The deeper message I wanted to convey to fighters with my tirade is this: The music you pick is not for *you*. When choosing music, do not select what *you* would like to hear or what *you* think will make you cool or special. I know you don't have the mental chops to come up with a list of priorities yourself, so Uncle Chael will provide it. When deciding on your walkout music, you need to consider, in this exact order:

1. The fans.

2. The event.

3. The quality and relevance of the music.

4. Your personal taste.

So now that I have gotten my point across—in the understated, respectful, sensitive style you have quickly become accustomed to—and we can agree unanimously that I am correct, perhaps we can spend a little time on the subject of good walkout music: what it is, what it means, and how to identify and access it yourselves.

Walkout music should be enjoyable to the ears, be appropriate for the setting, and convey a sense of the fighter's mission. It should have a good opening and then a buildup. It can't blast off at a hundred miles per hour like most bad metal because then it has nowhere to go. It just drones along, boring everyone to tears. Tempo wise, both too fast and too slow are equally lethal. Time changes are good (which kills all of reggae, thank God), but too many time changes become annoying. Remember how long you've got to walk, and find music that entertains and, seriously, do try to tell a story in that time frame and make a conscious effort to represent something *real*. Look for music that is original but not obscure, engaging but not oppressive, energetic but not hyperactive.

It should also be a big-room song, if you know what I mean. It should sound good in an arena, not just in your headphones. I love songs like "Operator" by Jim Croce or "If You Could Read My Mind" by Gordon Lightfoot, but they're not big-room songs. Two examples of big-room songs are "More Than a Feeling" by Boston and "Don't Stop Believin'" by Journey.

Just remember the vibe, the event, the nature of the spectacle, and the *context*. I will grace you with some suggestions, starting with a handful of good songs, and then concluding with Uncle Chael's Top Ten Hall of Fame Walkout Songs. Enjoy.

Good Walkout Songs
(Honorable Mention)

"Use Somebody" by the Kings of Leon.
Great opening. Great buildup. Great song.

"Girlfriend" by Matthew Sweet.
The late, great NY guitarist Robert Quine goes into hyperspace.

"Best of You" by the Foo Fighters.
Dave Grohl. Genius.

"Tired of Being Alive" by Danzig.
See, heavy is OK, kids, if you have an opening, a melody, and a *singer*. The first line—"Don't care if 'n' you die"—says it all.

"The Fuse" by Jackson Browne.
Just such a great opening—ominous and interesting. Just great.

"Ghost Symbol" by Zero 7.
Weird. Unique. Amazing.

"Lady Picture Show" by Stone Temple Pilots. Great opening. FYI: STP saved rock and roll in the '90s.

"The Song Remains the Same" by Led Zeppelin. Jimmy Page. Best ever. Bonham. Best ever. Song. Amazing.

"The Changeling" by the Doors. The opening song on the '70s masterpiece *L.A. Woman*. Not an obvious choice from Jungle Jim & the Boys, but just a great opening—hoarse, bellowing: bombed Lizard King at his best.

"What Is Life" by George Harrison. Again, great guitar opening, buildup, everything.

"Soul Makossa" by Manu Dibango. This is a 1972 saxophone song from Manu Dibango, a guy from Cameroon. It starts off dark and mysterious, with atmospheric conga drums pounding out a rhythm only the Dark Continent could produce. Next: whispers, mutters, chants, and ominous words. And finally the *blast* of a saxophone solo. The song is engaging, unique, enigmatic, and great. Older fans will recall it immediately; younger fans who have never heard it will be blown away.

"Hero Worship" by the B-52's.
Wow. Just WOW. Ricky Wilson, dear, departed guitar genius, played with only four strings and invented his own tunings. This song is on the B-52's first record, a masterpiece of brilliant, raucous, musical subversiveness, equal to "Never Mind the Bollocks" by the Sex Pistols and the Ramones' first record—all landmarks in the reinvention of popular music in the mid-1970s. This song got kind of lost in the sauce, with hits like "Rock Lobster" and "Planet Claire" dominating the airwaves and dance floors, but dang, it is an amazing song. Ricky's astonishing guitar duels with his sister Cindy's bizarre, amazing voice, until she simply shrieks the song, causing it to pull free of the earth's gravity and float around the cosmos. You wouldn't hurt yourself walking out to "Lava" off that first album, either.

"(It's a) Family Affair" by Sly & the Family Stone.
Great intro, and then Sly comes in, obviously zonked out of his mind on only God knows what. He totally blows the timing when he comes in on the second verse, which is hysterical and makes the song even better.

"Hold Me, Thrill Me, Kiss Me, Kill Me" by U2.
I include this song begrudgingly because Bono is such a self-righteous, pontificating wanker. But it just has such a great, great opening. The song is interesting and original—Big Room all the way. And to their credit, U2 had a big-room sound years before they were playing big rooms. So props. Now Bono, lose the welder's goggles, grow your hair out, and shut up once in a while, ya big windbag. I'll be back to torture you at some point.

"Your Day Will Come" by Cousteau.

This band from England had to change its name from Cousteau to Moreau after its first album, because of some legal issues with a bunch of French scuba divers nobody'd ever heard of that had rights to the name Cousteau. Whatever. This is just a great walkout song. The piano leads us into a doomed, bleak march, as Liam McKahey (what a *voice!*) solemnly intones "Your day will come/It's catching up on you" in his rich, silky baritone. Give this one a listen, kids. And, it's also a great song to *leave* to; as your opponent is laid out, a shambles of disappointment, regret, blood, misery, and despair, Liam croons "Hope rides another day. ..." Wow.

"The One I Love" by R.E.M.

Now *here's* an interesting choice. Great opening, great song—Peter Buck's jangling Rickenbacker, Michael Stipe's beautiful, uniquely American voice, and ... the subject matter, which is ... the *exact opposite* of what it is perceived to be. Think about it, kids. Especially you dopes who used this as a wedding song or a prom song or whatever. (Most of you are divorced and/or didn't graduate anyway, so that should dull a bit of the pain of what I'm about to share with you.) Stipe appears before us as a singer, but also, and more important, from a standpoint of criticism and interpretation, as what we call in literature (and lyrics are, occasionally, literature; read the lyrics to "Jokerman" or "Tears of Rage" by Bob Dylan, or "Powderfinger" by Neil Young) the unreliable narrator. Think about what he says:

This one goes out to the one I love
This one goes out, to the one, I've left behind
A simple prop, to occupy my time. ...

Do you see the callous insult implied by these seemingly adoring words? "I'm only thinking of you because I'm on the road,
and I'm bored!" And then, as if that's not bad enough, he con-
cludes by saying:

This one goes out to the one I love
This one goes out, to the one, I've left behind
Another prop, has occupied my time. ...

I just love, LOVE, the meaning
of the song, and it can't even
be called a hidden meaning.
It's right out there; you can
hear every word. It is a song
of such scalding contempt and
such cruel antipathy. But if you
really give it some thought, it's
not either our narrator's current
or previous "prop" he feels that
contempt and antipathy for—
it's *himself*. You fighters should
think about that as you slink up
to your rooms with your latest
MMA groupie.

The Ten Great
(in Ascending Order)

"You Only Tell Me You Love Me When You're Drunk"
by the Pet Shop Boys.
What a song. Listen to the opening. Then listen to Neil sing "What a performance tonight/Should I react or turn out the light?/Looks like you're picking a fight. ..."

"Saturday Night's Alright for Fighting"
by Elton John and Bernie Taupin.
This would be especially entertaining if the fight is on a Friday.

"You Could Be Mine"
by Guns n' Roses.
For all you fans of Gn'R who were ready to hang me from the yardarm a page or two ago, here's a *great* song. It's much better than "Jungle" in every way; not just as a walkout song, but as a song in general. Listen to them together. Compare and contrast. Acknowledge the obvious. This song just *kicks ass*. Try to time your entrance into the ring as Axl shrieks "Don't forget to call my lawyers with ridiculous demands!"

"Heads Explode"
by Monster Magnet.
The heads of the people in the crowd will explode too.

"Go With the Flow"
by Queens of the Stone Age.

What a song, and the single-best rock video in the history of mankind. Talk Uncle Dana into showing the video as you walk out; it is a masterpiece of sex and death. When the chick squeezes the blood out of a human heart onto her chest right on the downbeat, you see a genius filmmaker at work.

"Work to Do"
by the Isley Brothers.

Incredible opening, fantastic song. Remember what I said about picking a song that tells a story? Well, listen to this song. Imagine what you'd be telling the crowd.

"Killed by Death"
by Motörhead.

Lemmy, with his best Motörhead lineup, just destroys.

"Chinese Democracy"
by Guns n' Roses.

Yep. Another Gn'R song. About 100 musicians, three or four guitarists doing solos. The album this song is on became a much-delayed laughingstock, but this particular song is just amazing, with a brutal, killer opening. Listen before you give this choice a dismissive, smug little chortle. Then admit I'm right. This is one of the best Gn'R songs *ever*, and a great walkout song to boot.

"It Don't Come Easy"
by Ringo Starr.

Holy Mother of God, if you could ask for a better song than this to walk out to, I don't know what it is—except, perhaps, the next song on my list, of course. Great big-room opening. George Harrison, who wrote this song, playing a sublime guitar lead-in, and then, the words. When it comes to telling a story about fighters or fighting, well, what else could you say, in a few words, that could be clearer than "It don't come easy"?

God, I love this song! If I wasn't such a superstitious, patterned, inhibited, pathological wretch, I'd walk out to this myself. As it is, I tried desperately to have one of my idols, a fellow fighter, walk out to this. (I can't tell you his name, but let's just say it may, or may not, rhyme with "Candy Routure.") He's come out to different songs over the years because he isn't psychologically trapped in a dysfunctional marriage to a song he despises and is embarrassed by—like someone I know, whom I see every morning as I brush my teeth. I truly believe that if he had come out to "It Don't Come Easy" rather than whatever forgettable, puerile crap he walked out to when he fought that big ol' slab o' cowardice Brock Lesnar, he would have killed him. That lucky punch the bloated, brush-cutted Lesnar landed would have been deflected by the karmic energy of a song so closely aligned with Randy (ummm, I mean, that anonymous fighter, who changed the sport and is the most popular, inspirational fighter ever), his life, his work ethic, and his journey.

Which leads us to ... drumroll, please ... the grand champion of walkout songs.

"How Soon Is Now?"
by the Smiths.

The first time I heard this song I thought it must have come from another planet; yet at the same time I felt it had come from a portion of my soul I was afraid to access for fear that it would drive me mad. Easily the single-most original, astonishing, and brilliant song of the last quarter-century. It confronts and describes issues that fighters are the living, breathing incarnations and victims of. The song is a throbbing, relentless, inexhaustible welter of loneliness, insecurity, and morose self-pity, sonically crystallized and packaged, then disguised as a brilliant pop song. If fighters could be captured in a song, it would be *this* one.

Even the video is great. A cheesy attempt at art, it comes across as an insincere, self-conscious artifice. Shot in black-and-white, it shows the Smiths in concert at the height of their powers: Johnny Marr, the genius behind the music, playing the guitar, as a shirtless, skinny Morrissey pinwheels his buggy-whip-thin arms and howls in that bizarre, unique, minor-chord warble, "I am the son and the heir/of a shyness that is criminally vulgar/I am the son and heir of nothing in particular. ..." That's fighters, ladies and gentlemen. Not heroes. Just a bunch of shy, lonely, insecure basket cases that destroy themselves and one another for the benefit of total strangers, for a little money, and for the feeling of acceptance and approval, from people they will never meet. (I call it the "good little dog syndrome"). The song "How Soon Is Now?" succinctly encapsulates exactly what it is that motivates fighters. It tells the story of our journey. It is a brilliant, unique, fantastic song, and hopefully, someday, some fighter with more guts than me will have the nerve to walk out to it.

Last-Minute Addition

"Sun King" by the Cult.

I don't have any idea how this one got past me when I was making my Top Ten list; I just *don't*. This song was one of the cornerstones of my argument, one of my Best o' the Best, and in the hustle-and-bustle of writing, it somehow got "lost inna sauce," so apologies to Ian, Billy, and whoever is playing bass and drums in the band these days.

"Sun King" is simply *off* the charts as a walkout song. The build-up is insane; this organ fugue (courtesy, I have no doubt, of the great Bob Rock, their producer) leads us into Billy Duffy's guitar intro. This song is so good, as both a song and a piece of walkout music. It's so profoundly perfect, that I'm wedging it into the Top Five using a little *post facto* reverse engineering, and I'm shoving "It Don't Come Easy" by Ringo into the Number 3 spot, moving everything else down one. This makes "Sun King" Number 2 on my list. I'm listening to it as I type this. If this song isn't just the greatest walkout song (with the possible exception of Number 1, "How Soon Is Now?"), I don't know what is. Somebody *better* come out to this, and *soon*. Any up-n'-coming fighter out there, ya wanna make your mark? Wanna start standing out, like your big, mean ol' Unka Chael? Build yourself, and your entrance, around *this* song.

Don't Get "Testy" with Me;

or:

How I Beat
Anderson Silva
Worse Than Any
Man Has Ever
Been Beaten
but Lost to a
Lab-Coat-Wearing
Guy I Never Even Met

Yeah, it's that time, ladies 'n'gentlemen, when I give you the lowdown on how I soared to the dizzying heights of ecstasy for twenty-five minutes or so, and then tumbled, like Icarus aflame, into the wine-dark sea of depression, regret, self-pity, misery, and horror, all courtesy of two interrelated, and irretrievably stupid, mistakes. The first mistake was mine; the second "mistake" belonged entirely to someone else.

Before we get ahead of ourselves, please step into the cage with Anderson and me on the infamous night of August 7, 2010. See that crazy look in my eye? Look charged, don't I? There is good reason. By this point in my life, I've already been busted by the feds for a crime I didn't even know existed, much less was capable of conceiving, carrying out, and covering up for five years. I've lost my real estate license and can never get another one, but they'll give a chimpanzee one if he turns over a couple of properties a month. My political career has gone up in smoke, shutting off that potential career and revenue stream for life as well.

In about a year, I've gone from being a guy everybody was voting for to a guy who can't even vote himself. I've been shamed and disgraced. It doesn't matter that people knowledgeable of the inner workings of Oregon politics have ominously hinted that prosecuting me had nothing to do with one isolated, busted-ass-play of a real estate deal, but rather with taking out a young, charismatic, conservative (i.e., me) by foul means when fair means failed.*

So right now, standing in the Octagon set up in this arena in Oakland, I'm pretty much out of options. I'm out of real estate. I'm out of politics. I've got … *fighting*, and if that doesn't work out, well, then I've got … fighting.

And I just happen to be fighting the best fighter in the world.

I'm ready. I've trained hard. I'm not going to leave anything in the tank; I'm going to pour it *all out* on that weirdo Anderson Silva. *All* the pain, *all* the rage, *all* the dissapointment, *all* the helpless, blind fury. *All* the regret. I am going to channel all of it into the performance of my life.

And I do.

I fight like I've never fought before. I surprise him with punches. I *knock* him *down*. I fling him to the floor and beat him like a rented mule. He, the master of deception, trickery, and mind games, is getting deceived, tricked, and mind-gamed right out of his title. I hold him down and beat him. I beat him until my hands feel like they are going to turn to mush. Over and over my fists rain down on his unprotected head, and he lies there like a lab rat with a severed spinal cord, waiting to be put out of his misery. I wait, and wait, and wait, as I punch, and punch, and punch. I wait for the referee to *end* the carnage. I have already hit Anderson with more unanswered, undefended strikes than *anyone* has every hit *anyone else* with in the history of the sport.

I cannot understand this. I've seen a thousand fights. I know how many times you should have to hit a guy without him hitting back, defending himself, or improving his position to make a referee stop the fight. I've *exceeded* that amount by a factor of *five*, and still there is

---

* elec-tion \i-LEK-shen\ *n* 1a: the process liberals trust when they win, but attack as unfair when they lose.

no reaction from the referee. So I punch on. But a nagging fear begins creeping into my brain: Is this going to be another instance where I do everything *right*, and still get screwed?

My mind flashes back to working in the real estate office; trying to sell properties, trying to do a good job, being a "team player"—filling in the paperwork as I was instructed to, then getting a call from the feds. I start thinking about how I had to tell the kids I coach what happened, and how, because of it, I may not be able to coach them anymore. That society may decide I'm unworthy of their parents', and their, trust. My mind flashes back to being booked and fingerprinted, and emerging, blinking into the daylight, a newly minted felon.

And still I punch on. But I am growing increasingly puzzled and distracted by the amount of punches I've landed, the rules concerning undefended strikes, and why I have to keep hitting this guy *long* after they should have pulled me off him and given me his belt. The gnawing sensation that something unnatural is occurring again in my life is creeping, like a fungus, into my psyche. Why the selective enforcement? If he had hit me a third as many times, he'd be out of the shower and on a plane back to Brazil by now, with his belt still around his waist. And I'd be on the next train to Prelim-ville. Where's the justice? Where's the fairness? Damn, where is the referee?

Four rounds of *pounding*. I've hit him more times than Bonzo hit the drums in "Achilles Last Stand." Twenty minutes of one-sided pummeling.

The world is *mine*, in five minutes.

I look across the cage.

He's shot. He's blown out. All I have to do is stay away for five minutes. He's too tired to even chase me down. He's ruined. I have battered him out of the business. And yet, when the horn blows to start the fifth and final round, I fight on. I'm not a coward with an insurmountable lead looking to ride a bike for five minutes and leave town with a cheap "W," like a certain champion whose name may or may not rhyme with "Peorge St. Gierre." I came to *fight*. I *engage*. I don't want to run and hide—in the Octagon, in my country, or in my life. I fling him down again, hoping that I am also flinging away my own bad fortune, my own errors of omission and inattention, my own faults. I pound him again and again. My mind wanders to my dead father, to whom, on his deathbed, I made a promise that I'd win a championship. To my mom, in the crowd. To my friends, my supporters, to the people who run the wrestling program who said to me, "We don't care about the case, Chael. You belong *here*, coaching our kids. They're *your* kids too. This is your home, and we are your family." My mind wanders to this, and to many other things, as I fight in the waning seconds of the fifth round of the most important event of my life.

What my mind does not wander to, or register, is that Anderson Silva has been holding my right wrist with his left hand for about twenty seconds. By the time I register what's happening, it's already too late to fix.

His leg comes up and over my shoulder, squeezing my head like a vise. I begin working my escape, but it's a waste of time. By the time I come back to the here and the now, *here* is the wrong place, and *now* is the wrong time. It's over. It's done faster than it takes to describe. Go watch the video. I'm in no mood to relive it for you second by second. I never will be.

It all comes crashing down: all the prep, all the training, the game plan, the sacrifice. It's all … gone, like the real estate career, the political career. Down in flames I go, AGAIN.

The rest is routine. The sponsor's hat perched crookedly on my sweaty, lumpy head. The bleeding cuts. Buffer screaming. The fury and resentment at my own lack of attention at the worst possible moment. I silently consider IRT (idiot replacement therapy). I consider asking my doctor if he has some serum that will replace me, molecule by molecule, with a new, improved version of myself that's *not so stupid*, and that *pays attention* to the tactics of his opponent, who happens to be the *best fighter in the world*, whom you *shouldn't* lose to by *falling asleep* and *losing focus* while you're pounding him. Huuuuuge mistake.

Press conference.
Hotel.
Airport.
One big blur.

Home.

It'a baaaaaaaaad. I don't have to tell you how bad.
Then, the letter arrives from California:

Dear guy who just blew the biggest fight of his life, which he had won,

Your testosterone levels are too high. If you can read this entire letter before the male hormones hurtling through your cheater's bloodstream turn this paper into a crimson mist, consider yourself suspended indefinitely.

That's not what it said *exactly*, but that was the gist of it.

The California State Athletic Commission

First things first. I was *never* accused of, much less found guilty of, taking anabolic steroids. Anabolic steroids are synthetic chemicals that mimic various natural bodily secretions, thereby fooling the body into producing more muscle, or scar tissue, or other stuff. I'm not a doctor. Look it up yourself. The short version, which I kinda just gave you, should suffice to give you an idea of what steroids are, and to let you know, once and forever, that I did *not*, nor would I *ever*, take them to gain an unfair advantage in a fight. I was not accused of that, and that issue *never* came up in any proceeding. Any connection between myself, and my circumstances, and anabolic steroids, is the product of the fantastical, nonsensical, and ridiculous speculation that runs rampant on the MMA Web sites.

I was, and had been for some time, under a doctor's care for low testosterone levels, a naturally occurring male hormone. Low testosterone has nothing to do with virility, muscle mass, or endurance-related issues; it is merely a body-chemistry imbalance. It is extremely common, it is radically unrecognized and undiagnosed, and it is easily treatable with short-term, monitored injections of testosterone, known as testosterone replacement therapy (TRT). Low testosterone is a condition no different than sinusitis or athlete's foot; and, like those conditions, it is treatable. So, when my condition was diagnosed a long time ago, and my doctor recommended treatment, I of course took his advice—as I'm sure most of you would have done had you been in a similar situation. If I had not taken his advice, I would be a very sick man, but I don't feel like going into the details of my condition.

Knowing that TRT was perfectly legal in my situation, I went to the hearing to clear my name. I went with the knowledge that the banned list of substances in professional sports is extremely sensitive. Aspirin is banned. Nyquil is banned. Caffeine is even banned, but no one ever gets popped for it because it leaves your system in fifteen minutes. However, if you were to chug a vat of espresso right before your urine test, you would most likely get popped for caffeine. The point I am trying to make is that damn near everything is banned. Testosterone is not. It is legal in forty-six states.

I went to the hearing to plead my case to the California State Athletic Commission. What I didn't know until I was standing before it is that everyone on the commission is either a friend of someone in a high place, or a friend of a friend of someone in a high place. Like most, I assumed that the commission was composed of a group of individuals who worked forty hours a week, trying to keep the board regulated. In reality, the executive director had a couple of cronies in his office, and the full commission met only twice a year. The members are from all over the state. To make matters worse, they aren't all up to speed on the rules.

So I went into the hearing and showed them that testosterone was legal in their state. I pointed out that I hadn't broken any rule; instantly they all began looking around, bewildered. Instead of dropping the issue on the spot, they switched the argument to one of "disclosure." Now I am no attorney, but I am pretty certain you can't do that.

For example, let's say you charge someone with murder. That person comes into court and proves that he had nothing to do with the murder. You can't suddenly say, "All right, you bastard, you might not have killed anyone, but we are pretty sure that you were speeding on that same day, so we are going to charge you for that." If that happened to you, I am pretty sure you would be thinking, "Wait a second, I wasn't charged with speeding. I don't have time to prepare a defense for speeding. Truthfully, I have no idea if I was speeding or not. Let me go back and look at this. Let me sit down with my legal team, and we will come back to see you another day."

Needless to say, I was frustrated. They switched the argument from whether or not I was taking TRT to whether or not I had "disclosed" the fact that I was taking the therapy. Well, they still didn't have a case. I disclosed my testosterone use in California four different ways. I could prove three of them. Two of them were in writing, so there was no disputing that. Two of them were not only signed and dated by me, but also signed and dated by members of the athletic commission. So, there was no disputing the fact that we did in fact disclose the matter.

What happened then? The charges shifted again. It was no longer a matter of if I had or had not disclosed the fact that I was on TRT, but whether or not I had disclosed the fact properly. My disclosure was to the executive director, and it doesn't get any higher than that on the food chain, but apparently I should have disclosed that information to the executive director's doctor. I don't understand why I would need to share my private medical information with a subordinate to the executive director, but if it had been put it in a rulebook somewhere, I would have obeyed. But it hadn't. In any rulebook. As a result, I assumed that the commission just made it up on the spot.

The end result: I got a six-month suspension. Well, that's not the way it works, guys. If I cheated, then it should be a year suspension, and I would gladly serve my time. If you can't show me which rule I broke, then I should get nothing. For me to go in there and prove that they were wrong, and for them to split the difference with me, was ludicrous. Did I break a rule or didn't I? There is no gray area here. If I didn't break a rule, there should be no six-month suspension.

What I found out later is that in the history of the California State Athletic Commission, it has never been wrong. Never once have the members ruled against themselves. But what they did was wrong. You can't recharge someone on the spot without due diligence. So immediately I began looking into my rights as an American. What were my options? According to a certain attorney to the stars, my options were vast. He charges something like a thousand dollars an hour, but he agreed to take my case for free. He told me that what they did was illegal, and that California had no cap, which meant I could sue them on a tort claim. I could sue them for an endless amount of money.

But was that a viable option? As an athlete, my days are numbered. If I sat out the six months, I would be done with the whole mess and I could go right back to fighting. If I took the commission to court, it might be a year before I saw a judge. So it would take twice as long to prove my innocence. I wanted nothing more than to fight back, but with the commission meeting only once every six months, and with any objection to their charges regarded as a "throwing of stones," I decided to grin and bear it.

Then came the media. One reporter on ESPN blatantly lied. He said my testosterone levels were four times that of the legal limit. Once he did that, once he spoke that untruth, it became my reality. I have no idea where he got that "information" because the commission never said anything of that nature. Why? Because it wasn't true. If my testosterone was truly that high, I would not be competing in the middleweight division. I wouldn't even be competing in the light heavyweight division. I would be in the super heavyweight division. In high school, at seventeen years old, I wrestled for the state championships at 185 pounds. Now, I don't know another person who can say that he weighs the same at thirty-four years of age as he did when he was seventeen. Not one. If I were on that amount of juice, I would look like ... well, I would look like Jose Canseco. And for the record, I do not look Jose Canseco.

I understand when a reporter chooses to believe the government over the person being accused of doing something wrong, but the government never made the claim that my testosterone level was four times the legal limit. Naturally, I asked the reporter if he even knew what the legal limit was. I informed him that the legal limit for testosterone is so incredibly loose that it would be near impossible for a person to exceed it. I told him to ask any doctor. If any man were four times the legal level of the loose limit, he'd be dead.

Did that matter? Nope. The damage had already been done. A number of other media outlets picked up the story and ran with it. I couldn't blame them—it was on ESPN for crying out loud. They just assumed it had to be true. The reporter who made the initial blunder promised to make it right. How did he do that? Did he go back on camera and tell everyone that he had made a mistake? No. He wrote a small article on the matter.

I was unjustly labeled a "steroid monger" and a "cheater." That had become my reality, and I had two options. I could vehemently deny the allegations, but knowing what I know about the media, that would only cause them to write more articles and stories. None of them would give me the time that you, dear readers, are giving me in this book to explain myself. So to shut them up, I simply went with it. One reporter said to me, "They tested you at .7 and the normal limit is .6." I said to him, "Retest that. You must have caught me on a low day." It was like the kid you love to tease on the bus; you only bust his chops for as long as he gives you the reaction you want. By going along with the whole charade, I got them to stop talking about it.

The whole matter reminded me of a gentleman on Ronald Regan's cabinet. They loaded a bunch of garbage on his back, and it absolutely destroyed him. When he finally got his day in court, he couldn't have been more innocent. After his victory, he said something like, "Well, I've won the case, but now whom do I see about getting my reputation back?"

My reputation was ruined and the whole ordeal was absolutely humiliating. But the truth of the matter is that if I don't stick a needle in my thigh twice a week, my health will deteriorate. So I am not going to quit doing it, and I am not going to apologize for doing it. Being unjustly labeled a cheater hurts, but when the only way to eliminate that buzz word is to sacrifice your health, it makes your decision a no-brainer.

Epilogue

I did my time and I am done. Don't ask me what happened, or when, or really how. I truly don't know, and can't tell you. I'm fighting again. I haven't fought in California. I don't know if I even can, or would want to. I don't want to even ask, because I am certain that the "answer" will be a jumble of confusion-producing legalese, with no real answer, and I worry that diving into that rabbit hole again might leave me stark, staring MAD.

I can tell you this—the last time I breezed through the ol' Golden State, one of the commission big wigs who made my life a living hell was standing at a red light, looking a bit worse for wear, holding up a cardboard sign that said, "Will Suspend Innocent Fighters Indefinitely for Food (Junk Science = Evidence)." I owed him a stern lecture, and maybe a slapping around, but instead, I just rolled down the window of the limo my sponsor had picked me up in, handed the worn-out old codger a five-spot, and told the driver to lead-foot me and my babe to the House of Blues for the Gospel Brunch.

NEW DOES NOT ALWAYS MEAN BETTER

When did *new* become synonymous with *better*?

f you read this book from the beginning, as opposed to flipping randomly around every time you sat on the toilet, then you probably remember reading my chapter on ancient knowledge and are probably thinking, "There goes ChaCha, contradicting himself. He just got finished telling me old things suck, and now he is telling me old is better." Let me explain. I'm not talking about old forms of martial arts or old styles of dressing. In those cases, new is clearly better. But America clearly has an obsession for *new*. Just look at our desire (no, our *need*) to upgrade our iPhones almost as quickly as we upgrade our spouses (*Siri*-ously, you don't need to replace your iPhone every two weeks.) But just because something is new does not necessarily make it better. To ensure we are heading in the right direction, we need to compare and contrast. This is especially true in politics. Let's look at the progressive ideology of "change." People on the left immediately view "change" as being better than what came before it, simply by virtue of being different—that is, not the same.

No one has been a more vocal advocate of change than President Barack Obama. The man stole the hearts and minds of disenfranchised Americans with that single word. It was the greatest act of mass-hypnotism in the history of the world. With a snap of his fingers, a wave of his hand, and by uttering the word "change" seven hundred million times, the nation became transfixed, as if merely listening to the word would alter the world for the better.

Nothing really changed, but at least the promise of the rhetoric was fulfilled. Out with the old, in with the new: the progressive agenda is advanced, while the old conservative docket is put on the backburner. But how often does anyone stop to think, "Is the new thing really going to be better than the old one?" Traditional ideas, values, systems, principles, and even people get cast aside as the new wave of righteousness rolls ashore. The waves crest higher and higher with the shrieks and complaints of the American Left.

Among those complaining and shrieking loudest and most often is Bill Maher, a lefty political pundit masquerading as a comedian. On his show, Maher crowns himself dictator of America and then creates the "new rules" Americans must abide by, or else suffer the consequence of not getting to sit at the table with the cool kids. Every week Maher goes over his set of rules, cleverly disguised as punchlines at otherwise low points in the show, followed by a three-to-four-minute description of said rule in action, delivered in a manner that is half-comedy and half-seething vitriol.

But, again, are his new rules better than the ones laid down by our forefathers two hundred plus years ago as they framed our Constitution and the nation we have become? Does Bill Maher have some insight that eluded these great men, some of the greatest thinkers in modern history? Is it possible that the old rules were in fact superior to the new ones? Let's take a look at the old and new rules of charity, and I'll let you decide.

There was a time when charity meant that nice people put on their best smiles, came to you with hat in hand, and made their most passionate case for their cause. If you were kind enough, gentle enough, righteous enough, you may have offered up a few of your hard-earned dollars to help with their plight. Realizing the uncertainty of future funding, these people were exceedingly careful in how they spent every dollar you donated. Furthermore, society pitied these poor souls who required help. This made the recipients of charity hesitant about accepting the help and services of others, or at least cautious about abusing the goodwill of their neighbors.

Fast-forward a few decades. Now "charity" is liberal double-speak for "a group of people smarter than you are showing up at your house with guns, taking about half of what you earn, and giving it to their friends." Sure, some of it will go to the truly needy, but the bulk will go to the well-connected. And the rest will be used to create a permanent class of people who feel righteously entitled, not just to take your money, but to live a good life off it and simultaneously condemn you for living an even better life than they do. When charity is a choice, people's goodwill is divvied up equally among those they feel are the neediest. When charity is an obligation, the donors become jaded, the recipients become entitled, and the truly needy are often left out in the cold.

Don't get me wrong: Not everything old is better. Google is a better search engine than AOL, Cael Sanderson is a better wrestler than Farmer Burns, and Chael P. Sonnen is better than all that came before him. But in the immortal words of Issac Newton, "If I have seen further it is by standing on the shoulders of giants." For new to truly be better,

it must be based on using the wisdom of those before you, expand-
ing upon it, and coming up with something a step beyond. This holds
true for search-engine development, wrestling technique, or political
dogma. Ideas that worked in the past can work in the future. It's fool-
ish to throw the baby out with the bathwater, when a simple tweak to a
proven conservative formula could easily be the answer to the situation
at hand. We just need to stand on the shoulders of giants, not the shoulders of self-righteous people like Bill Maher.

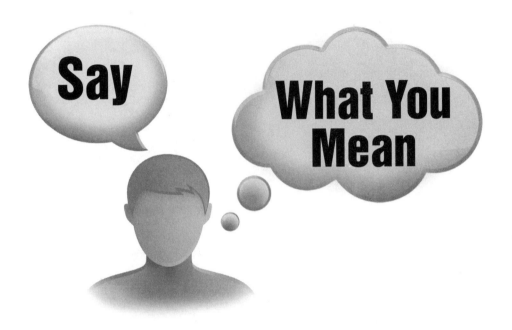

★ n my line of work I've heard it all, and frankly, I'm sick of hearing people say one thing but mean something entirely different. This is especially true in the world of mixed martial arts. To help you cut through all the mumbo jumbo, I will now offer my translations of the most typical lines you hear in the sport, and the true meanings behind them.

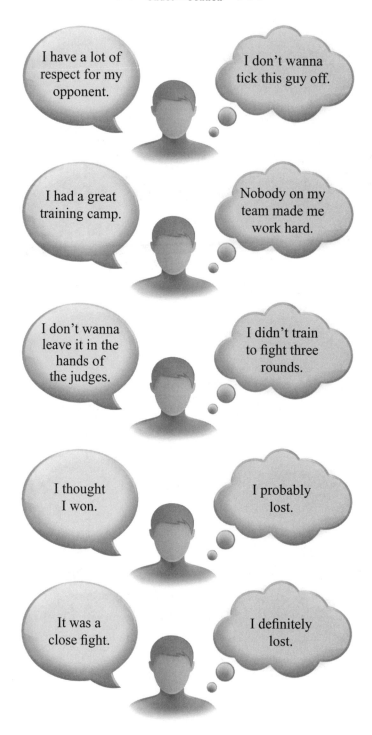

We're going to stick to the game plan.
We don't have the collective intellectual bandwidth to improvise, even if I'm getting killed.
This is a big fight for me, a big challenge.
Oh God, why did Joe Silva match me up with this guy?
I am going to knock my opponent out.
I really hope my opponent doesn't take me down.
My opponent can't match my skills on the ground.
I'm most likely going to get knocked out.
I'm a well-rounded fighter.
I can't do any one thing very well.

Don't Trust
Professional
Athletes

Back when I was a sociology major at the University of Oregon, I had two roommates, Kevin and Jessie. While I was busy studying and building my genius, they liked to play pranks on each other. Some were harmless, and others were rather vicious. One that fell somewhere in the middle took place on April 1 of my sophomore year. On this particular day, I walked into the kitchen to find Jessie brewing a disgusting concoction in a giant salad bowl. He started by pouring in a little milk, then he added some eggs. I didn't think much of it until he pulled a container of lunch meat from the fridge and started shredding it into little bits and dropping it into the bowl.

"What the heck are you doing?" I asked.

He said nothing, just kept a sinister smile on his face as he put a lid on the salad bowl and then poked small holes into the top, as if there were something in the nasty sludge he needed to keep alive.

I knew something was up, so I followed him as he carried the sloshing bowl to Kevin's room. I watched in amusement as he wedged the bowl into the narrow space under Kevin's bed. It wasn't until he removed Kevin's mattress and poked holes in his box spring that I realized the extent of his commitment. He didn't want Kevin to immediately notice the smell; he wanted the stench to slowly work its way up through his box spring, through his mattress, and then infiltrate Kevin's dreams.

I knew the punch line was going to take a while, so I went back about my business. So did Jessie. Sometime around the middle of May—six weeks after April Foolss Day—Kevin came into the living room and proclaimed, "My room stinks." I went in to investigate. His room didn't just stink—it smelled worse than a toilet in the slums of Mumbai. I had completely forgotten about Jessie's little prank. I was in the process of helping Kevin find the source of the stench when Jessie pulled me aside and reminded me about the little brew he had deposited under Kevin's bed.

At this point, Kevin had begun dating this very annoying, very mean girl whom both Jessie and I had a strong disdain for, so we joined forces and tried to convince Kevin that it was the girl who had made his room smell bad. "Dude, I think she has some issues," were among the words spoken. Kevin ignored us and, to the best of his ability, the smell. But it was finals week, and the smell in his room got so bad that he could no longer study. He washed his sheets every single day, sometimes twice a day. He vacuumed his floor incessantly. He wiped everything down in his room with disinfecting wipes. And still he couldn't get rid of the smell. Although it was mid-May, it was freezing cold in Oregon, and he had to sleep with his widows wide open. Unable to remove the smell by cleaning, he began to believe that perhaps we might be right about his girlfriend, and he broke up with her. When that still didn't get rid of the vile stench, he checked into a hotel.

The minute he left the apartment, Jessie removed the rancorous bowl and disposed of it. When Kevin returned from the hotel, the smell was gone. Needless to say, Jessie and I informed him that having the apartment free of his former girlfriend for five days finally allowed her stench to clear out. Remember, neither one of us wanted him to get back with her.

Although we kept what we had done a secret from Kevin, we didn't keep it a secret from our other friends. At the time, Ben Crane, the now-famous golfer, was one of our study partners, and he shared a good laugh at Jessie's shenanigans. We told him every last detail of the prank. We shot our mouths off far and wide, and we realized that it would eventually get back to Kevin. So on graduation day, Jessie handed Kevin a card inside which was a detailed description of the origin of the mystery smell that had permeated his room months earlier. As you would imagine, a very pissed off Kevin began chasing a giggling Jessie around the campus, confusing everyone in their Sunday best. That was the end of the matter. Jessie had a great story to tell his grandkids.

Fast-forward four years. Jessie and his wife were in town, and Jessie invited his old buddy Ben Crane and his wife out to dinner. At one point the conversation died down, and Ben's wife said to him, "Hey, tell them the story about what you did to your roommate in college. You know, about that prank that you pulled with the salad container."

"Aw, I don't want to tell that story," Ben said.

"No, you *have* to tell it. It is soooo funny!"

Ben looked across the table, right into Jessie's eyes, and said, "For April Fools' Day one year, I filled a salad container with a whole bunch of nasty stuff and stuck it under my roommate's bed."

"Really?" Jessie said.

"Yeah." He went on to describe Jessie's prank in minute detail. He talked about how he broke up pieces of turkey, and how his roommate dumped his annoying girlfriend and even moved into a hotel so he could study for finals.

Jessie didn't need a bullshit detector to know Ben Crane was lying, was retelling Jessie's story as if it were his. Apparently Ben had told the lie so often, he had completely forgotten that it was Jessie who had told him the story in the first place. Jessie, being a good guy, was going to let it ride. But Jessie had told his wife that story on many occasions, and she wasn't going to let it fly. Immediately she said, "Ben, you do realize that you are telling Jessie's story. You realize that he is the one who did that prank, not you."

I will spare you all the details about the havoc this caused at the dinner table, but let's just say that it was pretty freakin' hilarious: Ben's wife began screaming at him for lying to her for so many years, and Ben looked as if he wanted to run out of the restaurant. When you break it down, I guess there are several morals to this story. The first one is, Don't lie. And the second one is, Don't believe a word that comes out of the mouth of a professional athlete. Unless, of course, that athlete is Chael P.

That reminds me, did I ever tell you about the time I stopped a mugging the day I was to fight for the title. Yeah, it was Greg Jackson and me. ...

HISTORY
of Wrestling
and The Martial
Arts

Not much can be said about wrestling—other than it is the best sport in the history of the universe. It also happens to be a very old sport. Now, if you read my blurb on ancient knowledge, you know I'm not a huge fan of people who worship something simply because it is old and mysterious. People have done a lot of stupid things throughout history, and there are groups of people today who like to identify themselves with those stupid things, not realizing that they are even stupider now than when they were first practiced. If you look back through history, wrestling was one of the few things that people got right. How do you know? Just look at the class of people who wrestled.

In Egypt hieroglyphs engraved in stone circa 2500 BC depict athletes wrestling it out for supremacy. I'm not a big fan of Egypt, simply because of the buildings shaped like triangles there, and after my fight with Anderson, I have come to hate all things that have anything to do with that horrible geometrical form. But you have to admit that the Egyptians were pretty badass. Baquet III, Egyptian governor and wrestling fanatic, had 405 images of wrestlers chiseled onto his tomb when he kicked the bucket. In these scenes you can find double-leg takedowns and knee blasts. The Egyptians even wrote a list of rules and instructions on papyrus around AD 100, laying out all the aspects of wrestling training and competition.

The Egyptians weren't the only ones to wrestle for sport. Ancient Indian civilizations made mention of wrestling in their epic Sanskrit texts as early as the fifth century BC, and the Chinese used wrestling to keep their soldiers on their toes during peacetime. Even Genghis Khan, the super awesome Mongolian warlord and leader, was reported to have instructed his soldiers to learn the perfect trifecta of "the three manly skills"—wrestling, archery, and horseback riding.

Who knows how long wrestling has been around. In prehistoric times, all the real men were out wrestling sabertooth tigers, and all the liberal-arts majors failed to survive childbirth. It wasn't until we began coddling and subsidizing the liberal-arts wieners that articles were written about the sport. The bottom line is that for as long as men have had arms, they've been wrestling. To solve disputes. To stay in shape. To sharpen body, mind, and soul against any and all challenges they might face in their brutal existence. In short, every little society on earth that had two brain cells to rub together independently realized the great heights that can be attained by having the young men of their culture grab each other and toss each other to the ground.

Unfortunately, some societies did not have two brain cells to rub together. Unfortunately, some societies didn't even have one brain cell to rub against the empty space filling up the rest of their brain cavity. Against all odds, these societies were too stupid to invent wrestling or at least a reasonable facsimile. Instead, they developed a "martial art." In hindsight, voluntarily forfeiting their lives to slavery would have been a better choice for these cultures, as they have added very little to the betterment of the human race. Below I offer a brief description of these martial arts, allowing you to make up your own mind as far as their relevance.

Karate

When discussing pointless, time-wasting endeavors, karate has to be the second activity you consider (the first being trying to convince the California State Athletic Commission of your innocence). Karate was developed on the small Japanese island now known as Okinawa by out-of-work fishermen. Because of their humble position in the economic structure of feudal Japan, these malnourished fishermen began consuming their own urine to recycle vital nutrients missing from their meager diets. Of course Japanese society frowned upon this, and eventually the fishermen-turned-urophagists were exiled to the outskirts of society. To exact their revenge on Japanese society at large, these pariahs developed a unique style of martial art to perfect their minds and sharpen their bodies. Unfortunately, they were still extremely malnourished and quite easily broke their hand bones. They remedied this situation by swatting weak kicks at their opponent and then simply refusing to engage for hours at a time. This method would annoy most opponents into defeat. This style of pseudo-attacking and running for your life, called karate, was born, and Japan adopted it, and the fishermen, into society with open arms. In an effort to make the story more family-friendly, Japanese society buried the true story about the piss-drinking originators of the "art." However, once in a blue moon, before important fights, you can still find Japanese karatea drinking their own urine in an effort to connect with their forgotten ancestors.

Tae Kwon Do

Surprisingly, despite its humble origins as a coping mechanism for insecure Japanese salarymen, karate did have its imitators. Korea, aka, Japan Jr., also wanted a piece of the running-in-circles-while-randomly-throwing-kicks pie. Koreans will take any opportunity to rip off the Japanese and steal a part of their culture while vehemently arguing not only that they are its originators but also that they in fact do it better. This was the case when Korea imported karate, changed nothing, and called it tae kwon do. I'm fairly certain that "tae kwon do" literally means "avoiding copyright infringement." Because of the weak legal system in the Far East (so weak in fact that 94 percent of Korean lawsuits are settled by a coin flip), they managed to get away with this blatant theft. But if you look at the bricks and mortar of the arts, you'll see that tae kwon do is exactly the same as karate. Illegal face punching? Check. Thin, wispy gi to allow airy comfort in the crotch region? Check. A dizzying array of kicks so powerful they could decapitate a butterfly? Double check. Do yourself a favor: when trying to decide between taking up karate or tae kwon do, choose suicide instead.

Savate

Since we're on the subject of kicking arts, I have to mention savate. Indulge me for a moment and consider the consequences of this scenario: You live in early-nineteenth-century France. You are gainfully employed as a boot-shining apprentice working under a man who cleans horse manure from the filthy streets of Paris, and out of nowhere the king of England comes into your personal space and starts shoving you around. You've got on your big ass-kicker boots (shined to perfection). This guy is in your grille, giving you a hard time. And, most important, a closed fist is considered a deadly weapon in early-nineteenth-century France (yeah—I didn't make that up). What are you gonna do? The answer is obvious. Develop the lamest fighting style in the history of Europe, centered around kicking your opponent *exclusively* with your cool boots, occasionally releasing a quick flurry of slaps, and pretending you invented a martial art. News flash: kicking with your foot isn't a new martial art. It already has a name. It's called incorrect technique.

Muay Thai

If one nation of people knows how to a kick correctly, it's the Thais. They've practiced their trauma-inducing shin-bone-on-thigh-centric martial art for a millenium now. Legend has it that muay thai arose when the Burmese army kidnapped a Thai warrior. Khanom Tom, as he was known, fought his way to freedom by defeating ten straight Burmese opponents. The queen of Burma was impressed by his manliness, released him and gifted him with two beautiful Burmese wives—because that's what always happens in national genocides. If you win a few kickboxing matches, they let you go free. It's not like they would drag you through the streets with a rope tied around your neck for having the *audacity* to win one match against their soldiers, let alone ten. Anyway, from this obviously true story about some obviously true character in an obviously true war, the national sport of muay thai was born. A martial art in which two men stand in front of each other and trade kicks to the thighs/body until somebody drops. If any sport were a candidate for Mensa athletic competitions, this would be the one. Having a game plan is frowned upon. Moving sideways or disengaging garners negative scoring. Blocking punches (with anything other than your face) is outright illegal. The only legal/traditional way to fight in muay thai is to stand in front of your opponent like a moron, bomb kicks into his midsection, and occasionally (probably randomly), check a kick or two thrown by him. So thank goodness the practitioners (aka human punching bags) of this sport know correct kicking technique. Because, lord knows, if you take up muay thai, you'll certainly be absorbing a lot of kicks.

Boxing

At least in boxing you are allowed to properly avoid and block a strike. Boxing is a true thinking man's sporting contest. Not content with the no-holds-barred brawls dominating the streets of Scotland at the time, John Douglas, 9th Marquess of Queensberry, endorsed a new set of rules governing fights. "Fair play," as it was termed, dominated the landscape. No longer were men concerned with winning at all costs. Suddenly, winning as a gentleman was thought the highest honor. The rules encouraged gloves, a "fair" chance to get back up if you fell down from exhaustion, and short rounds to allow the men adequate rest for their weary bodies. Fast-forward a hundred years, and the gloves are now little more than decoration for punches so hard they can break through cement, standing eight counts give a concussed opponent a chance to wake up and take another beating, and the short rounds encourage all-out action for short time periods, subsidizing the knockout punch. Boxing, designed to be noble and sophisticated, became the surest way to develop traumatic brain injury. If you've ever had aspirations of dying in the ring, you need to do only two things. Take up boxing, and wait.

Capoeira

Perhaps the most logical thing to do then is create a martial art with the sole intent of hurting your opponent as little as possible. It seems that the Brazilians, in their infinite wisdom, have managed to do this with the creation of capoeira. Capoeira was a martial art developed by African slaves in Brazil during the 1700s. With fighting expressly prohibited, the slaves needed some way to resolve conflicts (that didn't necessitate an online grudge match via Battlefield III and an Xbox LIVE account). To keep their fights under the radar of the slave drivers, the slaves invented a time machine that would allow them to look three hundred years into the future at awful twenty-first-century teen movies. Drawing inspiration from great works of art like *Bring It On*, *Bring It On Again*, and *Bring It On: Fight to the Finish*, they developed their own dance-focused style of fighting to both beat one another to a pulp and annoy/confuse their masters. They expanded upon their dance-fight system until it became the well-rounded, intricately choreographed dance of death that exists today. No other fighting style (except for possibly every other fighting style) encompasses the depth of technique, the efficiency of motion, and the range of possible fight-ending attacks as capoiera's ritual of spinning continuously in the same direction while extending an arm or leg in a vain attempt to slap your opponent in the thigh.

If it's now obvious to you that striking is a ridiculous, futile endeavor (and it should be, because I'm laying it on pretty thick), then maybe you're thinking, "Uncle Chael, what about the other grappling arts? Are they awful too?"

Judo

The answer is yes. Judo is among the first attempts in history (but certainly not the last) for liberal-arts majors to develop a fighting style soft enough for their delicate hands but tough enough to earn them some street cred from their hipster friends down at the coffee shop. A Japanese hypochondriac by the name of Jigoro Kano watched some videos of the NCAA finals (wrestling, not basketball), and thought to himself, "How can I make this worse?" Kano succeeded in his mission by putting gi's on otherwise straight athletes, convincing them to go "easier," and babbling on about mutual welfare and benefit. He called this new art judo, and when the world rightly recognized that it was just a passive style of Greco-Roman wrestling with a jacket, he quickly and haphazardly allowed two types of submissions, as if that made any difference at all. This new art of judo even found support among the international community, gaining acceptance as an Olympic sport in 1964. This sport revolves around sloppily throwing your opponent while grabbing his shirtsleeves and, as far as I can tell, not much else. Some Olympic sport.

Sambo

Not wanting to be left out in the cold in terms of embezzling Japanese martial arts (all the cool kids were doing it), Russia decided to get in on the act as well. In the 1950s the USSR traded the Japanese government one year's supply of food for 5,000 Judo gi's. The Soviet geniuses then dropped the gi's out of helicopters over St. Peter's Square and watched with glee as mass hysteria ensued. Those who garnered a gi, and didn't die of starvation, became the first crop of Russian judoka. These autodidacts tried to master the intricacies of the Japanese art through osmosis. Unfortunately, because all the literate Russians were sent to Siberian work camps, the Russian practitioners had no clue what the actual judo rules were. Taking their best guess, they emphasized leg locks and disallowed strangleholds. Unfortunately, they guessed totally wrong. However, to save face, the Russians pretended that was their plan all along, and called their new leg-lock focused art form sambo. This small lineage of original sambo practitioners has spawned literally hundreds of thousands of sambokas who have gone on to accomplish absolutely nothing in the modern MMA scene.

Brazilian Jiu-Jitsu

But at least the Russians changed something. They paid homage to their foundational roots, acknowledging judo as their art's ideological forefather, switched some trivial points around, and tried to create something new and better. That's more than I can say for Brazilian jiu jitsu. The long, boring history involves a few members of the original Gracie clan learning judo from a legitimate Japanese judo teacher and, in the span of time it took him to go number two in the bathroom, renaming it Brazilian jiu-jitsu. Without changing a single technique, creating a single new rule, or inventing any new premise, the art was born magically out of thin air. A quick press release, a new marketing plan, and Brazilian jiu-jitsu was off to the races to dominate the martial arts world. To do this, the Gracie family (the original thieves of judo) developed a no-holds-barred fighting challenge to prove the superiority of "their" art. Royce Gracie's father (or cousin or something) created UFC 1 and filled up the tournament brackets with a bunch of washed-up, broken-down, stand-up fighters. Royce was then given the easiest route to the title as he tied up, choked, and tickled his way to UFC gold. The rest, as they say, is history.

The history of the decline of humanity, that is. Do these fools honestly believe they invented a new martial art? A new system of mutually beneficial, holistic combat? Bollocks. Mud-eating cave dwellers in the mountains of Kazakhstan were doing keylocks and lapel chokes a billion years ago. In short, wrestlers were doing it first, and they're still doing it better.

And it shows. In the character of the men who wrestle. In the hardwork and determination they put into everything they do. In their reverence for their teachers and in their refusal to take credit for what they had no hand in creating. Mostly, it shows in the men that wrestling creates. Everyone from Gen. Norman Schwarzkopf to Gen. George Patton to Maynard James Keenan. And almost every US president worth a hoot has had a strong wrestling pedigree. (Aside from Richard Nixon, of course, thanks to a misdiagnosis of tuberculosis and subsequent family boycott of all sporting activities. Had he not been affected by this unfortunate circumstance, he almost certainly would have won four Greco-Roman world championships and still become leader of the free world in his spare time.)

Here is a list of some great men:

★ George Washington (Independent)

★ John Tyler (Whig)

★ Zachary Taylor (Whig)

★ Abraham Lincoln (Republican)

★ Ulysses S. Grant (Republican)

★ Chester A. Arthur (Republican)

★ Theodore Roosevelt (Republican)

★ William Howard Taft (Republican)

★ Calvin Coolidge (Republican)

★ Dwight D. Eisenhower (Republican)

What do all these presidents have in common? Aside from their universal refusal to join that other political party full of crybabies and weaklings? That's right, all of these outstanding specimens of manhood were wrestlers. Maybe not world champions, but the hard work, full-bore training, and mental strengthening paid off by instilling in them the courage and tenacity needed to take on the highest political office, and win.

You can even take a look at the ranks of the UFC today and find that wrestling dominates the top of every single weight class. Nearly every UFC champion has a foundation in wrestling.

★ **Heavyweight:** Junior dos Santos (not a wrestler, but wishes he were)

★ **Light Heavyweight:** Jon Jones (wrestler)

★ **Middleweight:** Chael P. Sonnen (the wrestler)

★ **Welterweight:** Georges St. Pierre (wrestler)

★ **Lightweight:** Benson Henderson (wrestler)

★ **Featherweight:** Jose Aldo (soccer player: can't win 'em all)

★ **Bantamweight:** Dominick Cruz (wrestler)

★ **Flyweight:** Will soon be Demetrious Johnson, Ian McCall, or Joseph Benavidez (all wrestlers)

It doesn't matter if you want to become the champion of the UFC [fill-in-the-blank] weight division or champion and ruler of the free world, history has made one thing abundantly clear. You'd better know some wrestlin' if you wanna do it well.

A Moment to Laugh at Me

■ am going to take a momentary break from telling you how things should be and share with you an embarrassing story about myself.

When I was twelve years old, I went to my cousin Lowell's wedding. Lowell has a twin brother, Sid, and with the two of them being very close, Lowell asked Sid to be his best man and give a speech. When the time came, Sid turned to his new sister-in-law and said,

"My brother and I have been very close our whole life, and we have shared everything. We look forward to sharing you, too."

It was all very sweet, and the assembled guests immediately erupted into applause.

Fast-forward twelve years. My buddy Terrance was getting married, and he asked me to be his best man and give a speech of my own. Well, Chael P. hasn't always been the smooth-talking, quick-witted girl magnet he is today, so instead of coming up with an original speech, I decided to steal my cousin Sid's. When it came time, I turned to Terrance's bride and said,

"My buddy Terrance and I have been like brothers for as long as I can remember, and we have shared everything, so we are going to share you, too. See you tomorrow night."

I immediately realized the implication of what I had said. It wasn't sweet and innocent like my cousin's speech. I had basically said that within twenty-four hours I would be climbing into bed with her. Not to mention that my buddy Terrance, her husband, would be present. I didn't say he would be videotaping the whole escapade, but I might as well have. I hoped the crowd was too drunk to catch my unintended drift, but unfortunately they did. I heard a plethora of gasps, and even heard a glass break, as if the person holding that glass had just been struck with a fatal blow. I didn't bother to look to see if it was the bride's father.

When I got back to my seat, everyone was staring at me. My girl-friend asked me how I could say such a thing, and then turned away in disgust. I'd rehearsed the speech several times, and for reasons I couldn't fathom I had ad-libbed that last line. It was, without a doubt, the most embarrassing thing that has ever happened to me. I'm still mortified by it, to this very day. I can't even think about it without cringing.

Victimhood and Other Nonsense

■★ 'm sure all you folks remember when an audio clip surfaced a few years back of moody actor Christian Bale lambasting a crew member on the set of *Terminator Salvation*. (If you haven't heard it, it's worth a listen.) The clip went "viral," which is what I believe all you lil' geeks with your Interwebs and whatnot call it, and the consensus opinion assigned victimhood to the target of Bale's fury, director of photography Shane Hurlbut. After reading numerous comments and having discussions with my friends and cronies, all of whom love movies, it became apparent to me that Bale had been cast as a bully. He was generally regarded as a pampered lout of an actor who cruelly lashed out at a subordinate, a crew member who was "just doing his job."

Having been on a movie set or two, allow me to give you a slightly different perspective on the nature of the circumstances that created that particular incident and its resultant behaviors and impact. First, let's dispense with the notion that the subject of Bale's wrath was some poor workin' stiff schlumping across the set clad in a pair of Carhartt overalls and construction boots who just happened to have wound up in the wrong place at the wrong time in front of the wrong actor. No. He was the director of photography. He was the head of a department, a high-ranking member of the creative team; more "talent" than "crew"; more "management" than "labor." He *hires* guys to work for *him*, and he collaborates with the director (in this case, a hack and a complete fraud who calls himself "McG," whatever the heck that is supposed to mean) to envision, design, and create shots.

Prior to Bale's appearance on set, in wardrobe and makeup, the DP and his entire crew had full, unrestricted access to the set and all the equipment (in this case, lights), with the added assistance of a stand-in for Bale—an individual of similar size and approximate physical architecture whose one and only job on set was to sit where Bale would sit and stand where he would stand. All these luxuries were offered so that any "fine-tuning" and "tweaking," code words for "fixing my screwups, could be performed without disturbing Bale, so that when he showed up on set he could do *his* job, which is *acting*.

I can assure you that the DP was given as much time as he needed to accomplish his tasks. Rest assured, my fine friends and fellow film-fanatics, had the DP (or any of his mindless minions) been rushed or inconvenienced in any way, he would have howled to the AD (essentially the quarterback on set), the producer, his agent, his manager, etc. And he would have howled longer, louder, and with a lot less decorum than Bale howled at him.

Second, and this is vitally important—if you listen to *what* Bale says with the same degree of enraptured attention you give to *how* he says it, you will realize that this is not the first time this had been an issue. Bale makes it clear that the DP has already behaved unprofessionally and inappropriately, and someone, in all probability Bale, has already told the DP to stop walking around and adjusting the lights, which as we have already discussed, should not have required adjustment during a scene if the DP had done his job properly.

By now you are probably wondering why I am talking about this at all, and I am going to tell you. Because the DP manifests a behavior pattern that has become all too common in modern American culture, the characteristics of which include:

★ Laziness.

★ Incompetence.

★ Impunity.

★ Self-confirmance of victimhood status upon oneself as immunization against criticism.

Bale went to the set expecting Hurlbut to perform at a certain level of professional competence and with mutual decorum and respect. When that proved unrealistic, he took the step of discussing it privately (or, at least, in a less-incendiary and obvious manner than the recorded rant later caught). When that failed, Bale focused his righteous, warranted, justified fury at him. If I were a bettin' man, I'd wager my dear, old danglers that since that incident, that DP has his lights set and ready before actors are called to set, which means that:

Christian Bale's rant made him better at his job.

Think about that the next time you decide to let someone do less than his or her best so as not to "victimize" or "oppress" or "offend" him. You're not *helping* anyone by sparing his feelings and letting him get away with terrible work. When you allow stupid, lazy, incompetent, indolent people to make themselves into victims, you're shirking your own responsibility as a member of culture, society, and civilization itself.

> *So I want to take a step back and say, Thank you, Christian Bale. You made the world a better place.*

While writing this book, I have been experiencing a prolonged tingling, an obvious byproduct of Bale's do-goodery, and I want to let you know, dear reader, that every derogatory thing I say about you throughout this book is my humble attempt to make you better, make America better, and make the world a better place to live. I don't expect anything in return, other than perhaps a small thank you, which you will write on the last page of this book in permanent marker. And don't forget to include the "P," which as you know stands for "Perfection."

My Father

For the longest time my father thought I was on drugs. As I already mentioned, I didn't do anything in my youth other than go to school, attend wrestling practice, do chores at home, and sleep, but my father was from a different generation. On Sunday mornings I would sleep in until nine or ten, and to my father, who had woken at the crack of dawn his entire life, sleeping so late was a distinct sign that I was doing heavy narcotics. He never told me so personally, but he told my mother. I would wake up way after everyone else had eaten breakfast, head downstairs, and my mom would say, "Your father thinks you're on drugs." It didn't matter that I was a night owl and liked going to bed late on Saturdays, and it didn't matter that I actually got a lot less sleep than my father. If I wasn't up and ready to tackle the day before the roosters, there was a distinct possibility that I was hitting the crack pipe. Once I even went so far as to compare the number of hours that each of us actually spent sleeping. His answer: "That's what a drug addict would say." Anytime I missed a meeting, was two minutes late for something, or did a subpar job on some chore, it must have been for the same reason: drugs.

As you can imagine, whenever my parents went on vacation and left me at home alone, I went wild. And by wild, I mean I ordered junk food and shucked a few of my responsibilities around the house. Although I didn't realize this until I was twenty, my parents always came home from vacation one day early. If they said they would be back on the eighth, they always came back on the seventh. They did this every single time, and I never caught on. This resulted in me getting caught in all sorts of mischief, but one time was particularly memorable.

I was seventeen, and against my father's orders, I had used the twenty bucks he left me to buy a pizza. It wasn't that he was against me eating pizza; he just loathed the fact that I always ate one or two slices, and then stuck the rest of the pizza in the refrigerator without bothering to cover it, rendering it inedible the next morning. My father did not like waste. The next mistake I made was that I had forgotten to feed the horses for a few of the days my parents were gone. This mistake was quite large.

At the time I worked for my father's plumbing company, and a day before my parents were set to return from vacation, I was out on a job. I was fixing something under the sink when the homeowner told me I had a phone call. It was my father. Immediately the dried-out, barely eaten pizza flashed in my mind's eye. Something else bothered me as well, and then I remembered the horses. Things like this had happened before, and they had led to volcanic outbursts, but this time my father was unbelievably calm. "I'm home," he stated. "When you're finished, I want you to come back and bring a shovel and a pick with you."

Needless to say, I did not like the calmness in his voice.

That night when I got home, I was armed with a shovel and a pick. My father still did not say a word. He motioned for me to follow him, and we walked out into the neighbor's field. Pointing to the ground, he said, "I want you to dig me a ditch six feet deep, six feet long, and three feet wide." He didn't say he wanted me to dig a grave, but he might as well have.

And so I started digging; for the next three days I dug. The ground was so dense and dry, each pick swing resulted in only a minor chip of dirt. My hands became a rotten mess of blisters, and with it being July in Oregon, the sun drained my body of fluids. I must have been in that field for thirty hours combined, and although I came damn close to finishing the ditch he had requested, on the fourth day he signaled me to back away from the hole and then filled it in with the tractor. It wasn't until later that I discovered that once I had completely dug the ditch, he intended to build me a little bed inside it and have me sleep there for a week, subsisting on the dried-out pizza he had found in the refrigerator. He would have done it, too, if not for the blazing heat.

Just as with Roy Pittman, my wrestling coach, there was no room for excuses or irresponsible behavior in my father's world. When he made a commitment, he showed up and did the job right. It didn't matter if he was sick or hurt or tired. He expected the same from me. He expected me to do my absolute best with everything I touched.

A perfect example is when I lost my one and only wrestling tournament in high school. Afterward, he brought me home, pointed to a massive pile of rocks, and told me to move them across a swampy field. It proved to be the most torturous job of my life. I piled the stones in a wheelbarrow, but I couldn't get more than a foot through the marshy terrain without the stones spilling back onto the ground. I would then have to reload them and push them another foot. When I finally completed the job, my father came out and said, "Good job. Now put them back where you found them." I did, and we never talked about me losing the tournament again. I also didn't lose another tournament until I was in college.

My father taught me values that are largely missing in today's world. He was strict, yet he was also surprisingly lenient about me breaking certain rules. For example, one time I got into a fight with a buddy of mine in the school cafeteria. He ended up throwing a piece of food at me, so I sprung on him. I had never thrown a punch in my life, so I took him to the ground, controlled him, and then did my best to squeeze the life out of him. Neither of us got hurt.

We made up shortly thereafter and even finished lunch together, but then the teachers found out, and a short while later the principal pulled us into his office and called our parents. Now, my father didn't miss work for anything. When he turned up in his work clothes, covered in glue and dirt, I knew I was in serious trouble. And of course the principal didn't tell the whole story about how my friend and I had made up after the scuffle, and that no actual punches were thrown. She simply said that I got into a fight in front of the students, causing a massive disturbance.

My father didn't say a word as we walked to his truck. As a matter of fact, he didn't say another word until we pulled into the parking lot of a 7-Eleven. As I mentioned, I lived in the country, and there are no 7-Elevens in the country. So for me, 7-Eleven was the equivalent of Chuck E. Cheese to other kids. I thought maybe he would punish me by buying a bunch of treats and then eating them in front of me, but instead he said, "Let's go inside. You can buy whatever you want."

Alarms began sounding in my skull. What type of trap was my father trying to set? Hesitantly, I went inside. Again he told me to get whatever I wanted. Not sure if this was some type of test, I grabbed myself a Reese's Pieces and headed toward the counter.

"Wait," he said. I turned back toward him with wide eyes, waiting for the hammer to fall. "You sure you don't want a Big Gulp?"

He stood there, waiting for me to get one. So that's what I did—I grabbed a Big Gulp to go with my candy bar, certain that I would never get to sample the deliciousness of either. Again I started heading back to the counter, and again he asked me if there was anything else I might want. This was going too far! But he just stood there, waiting for me to gather more goodies. So I inched over to the counter and grabbed myself three or four corn rolls and a hot pretzel. With this, my father seemed satisfied. He paid our bill and we walked back out to the truck.

I didn't dig into my treats right away. I held back, waiting for some speech about how I was a drug addict, which would quickly be followed by him reclaiming my goodies. But that never happened. My dad simply drove the truck in silence as I ate and drank.

Later that night, as I lay in bed wide-awake, I heard my father talking to my uncle on the phone. Instead of talking about how his lazy, drug-addicted son had gotten into trouble at school, he was bragging about how I had gotten into a fight. Right then I learned a very valuable lesson—I couldn't slack on work or order a pizza that I didn't finish or forget to feed the horses. But it was A-OK if I fought. Perhaps this explains a little bit about how I ended up in my current profession.

My father meant the world to me. He was strict and as tough as nails, but he taught me about what really matters in life. I remember the day my mother told me he had cancer and wasn't going to make it. He didn't want anyone to know, so when I was around him, I had to pretend that everything was all right. You can imagine how difficult this was. Finally, he decided to tell me on his own, but after talking it out, he immediately told me to get the heck out of the house. I ran outside, climbed into his brand-new truck, put my head on the steering wheel, and began to cry.

Engrossed in my own world of misery, I didn't hear him come up to the truck. All of a sudden, I heard his voice in my ear. He didn't say, "It's going to be all right, son" or, "Make sure to take care of your mother." Instead, he said, "I see you are admiring your brand-new truck."

I pulled my head off the steering wheel, looked into his smiling face, and instantly realized what he was saying. We both began to laugh hysterically.

What a wonderful man. I love you, Dad. Rest in peace.

A False Sense *of Security*

★ n fighting, as in all things, one of your most forceful weapons is your ability to bestow a false sense of security on your opponent. More than punching power that causes a man's eyeballs to trade places, more than the reflexes of a greased-up French Canadian (and I mean this in a *very* generalized and nonspecific way), some of the greatest value in conflict lies in being able to feign so convincingly that the schmuck squaring off against you assumes victory before he has it. Then, while he is whistling "We Are the Champions" in some tinny, drunk dialect of Portuguese (another generalized, nonspecific example), you drop the act and hit him with everything you have. He will never see it coming; if you do it right, he will still be thinking about his victory meal when some bargain basement medic slaps him awake like a Victorian woman in the middle of a bout of hysteria.

Luring someone into a sense of complacency is both simple and artful. It requires subtlety, an understanding of your enemy's basic behavior, and a reasonably functioning set of critical thinking skills (three strikes, Lyoto; tough break). I am not talking about reverse psychology, which is simple enough to figure out and gets you only so far before your nemesis catches on. Reverse psychology is the mere act of using words and behavior to imply that you want the opposite of what you really want, without a whole lot of art or manipulation.

Sticking with just the reverse-psychology game is manipulative and condescending, and assumes that the person you are trying to deceive has the mental capacity of Sidney Crosby after that sixteenth concussion. The tactic works great if you are squaring off against a high school student, a drunk, or virtually anyone who watches *Portlandia*, or if you are using it as a one-shot strategy. If you are up against someone who has even the faintest twinkle of common sense behind his eyes, or if you keep repeating this move, someone is going to catch on to your game plan. When that happens, suddenly you will be the one who is lured into a false sense of security, and at that point you deserve whatever equivalence of a penlight gets shined in your glassy eyes. Play this card sparingly and randomly or only if you are very, very, painfully bored.

The simplest way to lure someone into a false sense of security is to play every card you have very close to your vest. In my industry you can't get anyone to shut up, from the champs to the scuttling little newcomers who just got off the bus like wide-eyed Kansas preachers' daughters with dreams of becoming actresses. If you shut up about what counts, you have power.

★ Do not give away exactly how you prepared, what you are expecting, what you intend to do, or where your strengths and weaknesses lie. If you do, you might as well draw your opponents a perfectly scaled map of Victory Lane. If they don't know what you have going for you, they will have to guess, and eventually they'll guess wrong.

★ There is more to keeping your mouth shut about your game plan than just keeping the other guy guessing. In fact, a very underrated tactic is simply coming off as weaker or less capable, the old rope-a-dope. Few things are more entertaining than watching a David beat a Goliath, but it's even better when David turns out to be an even meaner, stronger, more vicious badass than that punk Goliath ever was. This is because we love to watch the pompous morons get their legs knocked out from under them. Call it the broken-bird routine, or a wolf in sheep's clothing—call it whatever you want. The approach has merit, and proves especially funny in my industry. Case in point: Remember when BJ Penn shredded the "great" Matt Hughes into taco meat in thirty-odd seconds? The defense rests.

★ It never hurts to throw in a feint every now and then. This relates to reverse psychology a little, I guess, but is much better friends with good old-fashioned deception, straight up, without ice. My crazy Irish friend's even crazier Irish father always says that you should be able to tell the truth so outlandishly that it comes off like a lie, and then tell lies with a straight face so they have to believe you. I don't know if I would go so far as to agree with him, but he's absolutely right. (See what I did there? Of course you didn't.)

★ Dodge questions about what will eventually be your most venomous weapon, or at least downplay them. Change your tactics completely in midstream to keep them guessing. For example, say you hypothetically explain in detail how you prepared for an upcoming fight by going to Brazil, even though you never went. (I would never do that.) It's a trick favored by politicians, talk-show personalities, and virtually everyone who wants to get the best of anyone else. If done right (that is, done the way I would do it if I used this trick), it will work brilliantly on your opponent.

★ Don't think that you have remained immune to this feint in your everyday life, either. I promise you, nearly every person you love to watch on television is as in-character as any WWE wrestler at a sold-out arena on Pay-Per-View night. If you begin any thought about these people with, "he seems like a really nice and genuine person," then you are his favorite breed of fool. You're the type who still believes in Santa Claus and fad diets. You are our favorite sort of turkey. I mean, *their* favorite sort of turkey. Because I'm not like them at all. I would never lie to you. Trust me, because I am the real deal, and we are going to be best friends forever.

Santa

★ 've heard that self-deprecating humor is the best way to capture people's hearts, so I am going to tell you another rather embarrassing story from my childhood. I believed in Santa Claus until I was twelve. That's right, yuck it up. But before you start judging my aptitude, I want it on record that I felt something amiss four years prior.

At school, my sister and I heard other kids talking about how Santa wasn't real, so we decided to set a trap to find out once and for all. Every year about a month before Christmas, presents would start showing up underneath our tree. All these presents were from our parents. Well, on Christmas morning, a new set of presents would arrive from Santa,

but instead of placing them under the tree, he would place them on our chairs. He would put the presents intended for my sister on the chair she had picked, and he would place the presents intended for me on the chair I had chosen. Well, on Christmas Eve when I was eight, my sister and I told our parents that we decided to switch chairs. We had picked our chairs out months in advance, but the night before the big show, we told them that we'd had a change of heart. When we went upstairs, we looked up to the ceiling and told Santa to disregard what we had told our parents—that if he indeed existed, he should place the presents on the chairs we had originally chosen.

The next morning we came flying down the stairs. Sure enough, Santa had disregarded what we had told our parents. It was proof—irrefutable proof—that Santa existed. When the holidays were over, I returned to school and told all the naysayers that they could stuff it. Santa was real, and I refused to listen to anything to the contrary.

I held on to this belief for the next four years. I had seen news reports that covered Santas at local malls—they were fakes. I heard adults talking about how they had once believed in Santa—they were idiots. I had seen a drunk Santa's beard fall off at a bus station—he should be strung up for mocking the God-like figure who brought me presents every year. I held on to Santa like he was my security blanket, straight into puberty. And then came the fateful day when I just couldn't ignore all the evidence any longer.

"Mom," I said one afternoon, "if I ask you a question, do you promise to tell me the truth?"

"Why sure, honey," she said.

"I mean like promise-promise?"

"Yes," she said. "I promise."

I looked up at her with big, hopeful eyes. "Is Santa real?"

She hesitated for a moment, and it was the longest moment of my life. Then came the words. "No, sweetie, Santa isn't real."

My bottom lip, which was already growing a healthy amount of peach fuzz (remember, I was *twelve*), began to quiver. My defense mechanisms shot into overdrive.

"But years ago, we told you we switched chairs, and Santa got it right!"

"Oh, honey, your sister and you had your chairs picked out for months. When you told us you had changed chairs, we knew it was a trick."

Upper lip doing the jitterbug.

She looked down at me and smiled. "Do you want to cry?"

"No," I said, my voice cracking.

"It's really OK if you cry. I cried when I found out."

Yeah, there was only one minor difference. I was *twelve*!

Did tears start gushing down my cheeks? Did I run upstairs, jump under the covers, and sob into my pillow? Some things are better left unsaid.

The whole event proved so traumatic that I feel duty-bound to dispense with a few other myths that mess with the minds of my fellow Americans. Here are the facts (sorry to break it to you, but someone had to do it):

★ The Easter Bunny does not exist.

★ JFK was not a good president.

★ Yes, the earth is getting warmer, but it is called summer and it is not your fault.

★ The tooth fairy does not creep into your bedroom and put money under your pillow.

★ Liberal men do in fact urinate; they just use the stalls because they have to pee sitting down.

★ Once and for all, training with a gi does not make you a better fighter.

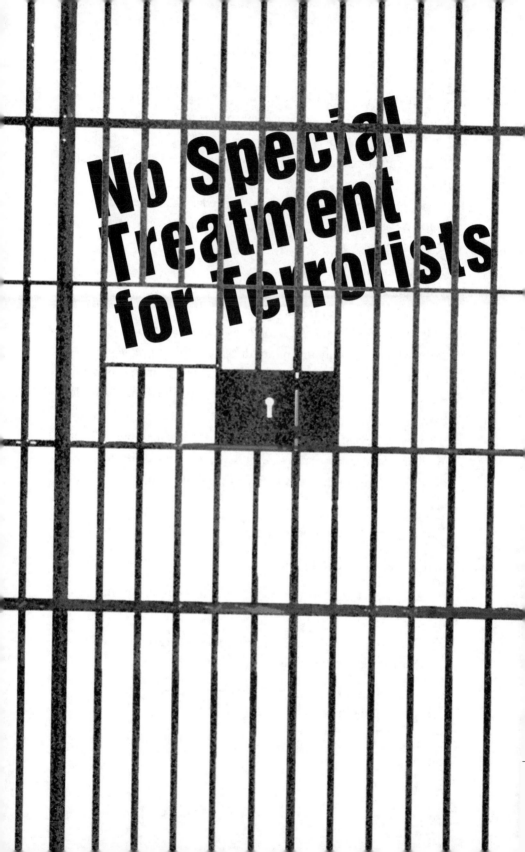

'm sure all of you have been patiently waiting for me to cover the topic of terrorists. Or, more important, what we should do with them once they are captured. The general consensus is that terrorists should be treated as enemy combatants, and dealt with accordingly. In an ideal world, this would mean swift military tribunals that are hopefully followed by even swifter death. But with many of these terrorist tribunals getting delayed because of red tape, and incarceration more hospitable than the terrorists deserve, I think there is a far better way of dealing with this scourge.

First off, terrorists are *not* in the military. They don't represent a country or a national or political will. They don't wear uniforms, declare war, or restrict their aggression to military targets, and their aim is not the acquisition of land or resources. Because of this, and the fact that they do not engage in combat, they don't deserve the appellation "enemy combatants."

What are they if not enemy combatants? They are criminals who target the weak, the unsuspecting, and the innocent for murder, by the cruelest possible means. With such a modus operandi, they do not merit the status of "prisoner of war" when they are discovered, dragged out of their filthy holes in the ground, and brought to detention centers. It does not, and should not, afford them the special privileges of private cells, huge security details, and a public forum for their beliefs. It does not, and should not, entitle them to the lead story on the evening news.

They should be greeted as what they are: murderers, gangsters, and cowards. They should be brought into whatever jurisdiction they are apprehended in, and then handcuffed to whichever scumbag got arrested right before them. They should be forced to sit on the floor of a holding cell that reeks of urine and sweat. They should be ordered around by corrections officers. In light of their probable history of cultural violence toward women, the toughest female CO, with a butch cut and a neck tat, should drag them, chained and helpless, into court and point to exactly where they should sit. If they refuse, then she should drag them there by their leash. She should stand behind them, and over them, to shame them, in their humbled, foul, urine-stained state, in every photo of them on trial.

The terrorists should be forced to exist in gen pop. They should have work detail like every other inmate, and no more access to visitors than any other convict, and every request for interviews should go through the regular system in the prison. They should get the bejesus beaten out of them over a vanilla pudding or a paper cup of Kool-Aid by some weight-pile gangbanger. They should get no special privileges, no high-security lockdown motorcade with hovering helicopters every time they have a court appearance. They should get transferred around the system from one hellhole to another, just like every other felon. They should spend their days with people just like them—vicious, brutal cowards—and be at the mercy of anyone stronger than themselves. They should be ordered around day in and day out by officers who have no respect or fear of them, who treat them with antipathy and disgust.

Whaddya think?

We've
Come
This Far

Chapter

'm being squeezed and forced down a dark, pulsating tunnel of living flesh. I've been ripped from a place of comfort and quiet solitude, a haven where I floated, with time suspended, for ages. The convulsive, relentless actions of a power I cannot control force me further and further toward my future, toward my fate. I feel crushed, malformed. My eyes are slits. I can see vague shapes, and discern dark from light, but barely, and only with effort. My ears feel clogged. I can hear, but like my vision, my sense of hearing is corrupted, semi-formatted, incomplete. I can feel, and at the same time I am numb. The forces that control my progress cannot be resisted or bargained with. There is no reason, no sense of humanity or concern, just that inexorable force pushing me ever onward.

I am wet, slick, greasy. I see light and hear voices. Hands grasp for me. I am grabbed, and thrust into the grasp of the unknown. A sharp slap brings me fully into existence. I open my mouth to scream. ...

Birth? Death? My Ring-walk?

All of the above.

You're never ready. You prepare. You train. You plan, plot, scheme, connive, accommodate, gather intelligence, float falsehoods to throw your opponent off the trail and identify moles in your own camp, encourage and nurture unholy alliances, sweet-talk sponsors, infuriate your family and friends, grind yourself into a fine powder day in and day out, then reconstitute yourself in the morning with water and hope, like instant mashed potatoes served in the soup kitchen of your mind.

You tell yourself you're ready.

Your cornermen scream it in your ears as you hit mitts backstage.

Your friends and family tell you you're ready, cell phones, granola bars, and energy drinks clutched in their hands. They are confident, but if you look closely, the hands holding those objects are trembling, ever so slightly.

You know you've done the work, but it's not the Angel of Knowledge you need right now; it's another, much more elusive angel in the canon whose intercession you urgently need. The angel we call Belief.

You're *never* ready.

But, eventually, inevitably, immutably, you're …

Next.

When Bert Fields, the captain general at UFC events, calls your name, you take that walk, ready or not. And as you do, as you take that walk and hear that crowd and listen to the familiar strains of your walkout song, as you and your cohort, wearing sponsor's T-shirts and hats, heads to the ring, you silently pray that the Angel of Belief will alight on your shoulder, smiling sweetly, chubby and rosy-cheeked, like Cecco, Caravaggio's model and muse, eyes alight with the wonder of possibility, full of secret and divine knowledge, shamelessly nude, like in the masterpiece *Love Conquers All.*

You wait, and watch, and listen for the Angel of Belief as you walk through a crowd of screaming strangers toward your fate.

And in a movie, if this *were* a movie, that angel appears, parting the beams of the seizure-inducing strobe lights as they flash in time to the walkout music you hate, but are stuck with because your sports psychologist believes in *routine*, even in a sport that lives and dies by *improvisation* and *adjustment.*

And sometimes the Angel of Belief appears.

But sometimes the angel ...

Doesn't.

But you still have to fight. The cage door is closed behind you whether you, your cornermen, your family, your fans, or your angels are ready or not.

So here we go. Down to the Octagon.

It's like looking through two paper-towel tubes, a kind of tunnel vision. Whatever is on the periphery disappears. Things in the center of your vision are in clear, sharp focus. You hear the referee ask you about your mouthpiece and groin protection. You grimace like a chimpanzee warning away potential rivals for a mate, and knock on your crotch like a traveling salesman behind on his monthly quota.

Your cornermen pull off your shirt, which inevitably gets stuck halfway off your head, and you clumsily struggle with it in your MMA gloves, your hands wrapped too tightly or too loosely, or both, or neither. You absent-mindedly wonder why no sponsor has come out with a shirt that has *snaps* up the front, like a hospital orderly's shirt, instead of the same horrid, rock-concert-quality shirts with the tiny neck hole and single-stitch sweatshop construction (that is, of course, everybody else's sponsor shirts; my sponsor's shirts are of the highest quality, are made for years of comfortable, reliable wear, and can be treated as objects of heirloom-quality pride and value).

OK, shirt's off. The officials point me to the stairs, like they're afraid I'll make a wrong turn, walk into the crowd, and start pounding a fat guy from Orlando here in Vegas on a UFC vay-kay. I'm usually pretty good about knowing where to go once I'm almost completely naked, covered in sweat and grease, in a room full of people chanting my name—and I also know where to go when I'm fighting.

So off I go, ready to stand, by myself, rather awkwardly, listening to someone else's walkout song, shifting impatiently from one foot to the other like an old gambler at the dog track with a hot tip, in a long line with a slow cashier a minute before the bell rings and the mutts start chasing the electric rabbit.

Here he comes. I watch, impassively, as he makes his way through the same fleshy tunnel full of grasping hands and blinding lights that I just negotiated. I begin manning the garrison in my own mind; the creaking, leaky fortress where I attempt to safeguard my confidence, where I try to immunize my insecurity by locking it in the deepest recesses of the stockade that is my inner psyche. But the troops I have left to defend the fortress are the least reliable; they are the last line of defense, once the best and brightest of my mental war-party, but they have been decimated by my training camp, previous fights, self-doubt, want, misery, pain, and regret. I survey this ragtag force; their armor is rusty, their weapons are worn and dull. Some have no weapons at all; just a steely-eyed stare, a mute, desperate resolve to serve, even if the campaign is doomed. Among them I see rheumy eyes, missing teeth, scarred visages, missing limbs. But still they stay and man their posts. I gather them together one last time. I attempt to give them my "Crispin's day" speech about how lesser armies have conquered more powerful foes, about how courage and faith can carry this day.

But *damn* that guy looks big.

And *damn* he's got a helluva walkout song.

And *damn* do I wish this were *over*.

And it will be … but not for a while.

Referee asks if I'm ready. It's too late to give him the spiel I just gave you readers about angels and Cecco and Caravaggio and all that. I don't think the referee, the deranged, raving crowd, or the massive PPV audience, all worked into a lather, are all that interested in my drama-queen, self-pitying poetics right now. And the big doofus across from me just nodded his head yes like a bobble-head dog on the dashboard of Granny's '64 Plymouth Valiant going down a bumpy country road, whilst saying nary a syllable, and I don't think he's too keen on waiting.

So off we go.

There are a few things I know.

I know it's gonna hurt. And I know I'm gonna bleed. I always do.

That's part of the occupational hazard of doing business, like the burns on a chef's hands or the needle tracks on a rock star's arms; it's just part of what a day at the office is all about.

And *what* an office!

I'm in the middle of the Octagon. I'm executing my game plan. He's backing up. He's waiting for the tackle. He's trying to line up his intercepting knee or shoot his hips back by springing backward from his toes up, removing his thighs and hips from the ballistic equation I am formulating in my wrestler's mind. But his plans form a self-defeating, desperate calculus; if he throws the knee and misses, he'll be perched awkwardly on one leg. Not the graceful, powerful, unbeatable one-legged stance of the legendary MMA fighter Ralph Macchio in *The Karate Kid*, but rather a sloppy, unbalanced disaster area awaiting the cleanup crew, also known as *me*, who will grab his off-kilter body and hurl it to the mat. Or he can sprawl, which will leave his head sticking out like a turkey on the last Thursday in November, anticipating the ax blow of my newly minted left hand, the mirror image of Henderson's right hand. My opponent has very little time to choose, as I advance, in perfect balance, hands up, changing levels, feinting. ...

He wants to initiate; his cornermen exhort him to "be first!" And he *will* be first—first to get tackled, first to get dumped, first to get immobilized, first to get punched, first to leave when the bell is rung for the last time.

I'm evolving as a fighter. I'll be the first to admit that many of my previous fights were predicated on a strategy that entailed a long fight and a decision win as my only genuinely realistic positive outcome. I had no hands. I had no submission skills. I was a wrestler. I concentrated on my strengths, and trusted them to carry the day. Even now, even as I grow and try to expand my skill set to include other techniques and tools, I know that when the pressure mounts, I, and everyone (you readers included), will retreat to the comfort of the familiar, which, for me, is wrestling. My objective right now is to present my opponents with scenarios that allow me to win, and win decisively and dramatically, while avoiding the necessity of the comfort of the familiar. It's nice to know that I have wrestling, much as it's nice for a riverboat gambler to know he's got his two-shot Derringer, but I'm working on acquiring other weapons so that my opponent becomes at least as confused, insecure, and scared as I am. If I can re-level the playing field based on the terms of my inadequacies, then I'm pretty sure my training, my skills, and my long history of wrestling can be the last card I play, if I need it.

So I feint. I watch to see what he bites on. Does he plant his lead foot flat to throw the knee, or does he slightly raise the heal of his lead foot, his toes pressed out and down, ready to propel himself backward into a sprawl? Do his hands drop? How much? Which hand?

And then buh-*bomb*. I throw the double jab.

He eats it; a look of bewilderment on his face. Thas right, suckah. ChaCha's got some *hands* now. He's got some better coaches and some better strategies. My boxing coach, Clayton, has been amazing. He should be working for NASA. He's turned this pumpkin into a horse-drawn coach, conveying my opponent to a place called Lump Town. Yep. Buh-*bomb*, the two jabs land again. Lumpy brings his hands up; *enough of that*, his body language eloquently says. He throws his own double jab, a predictable attempt to serve me with my own sauce, to pay me back in my own currency. To generate and deliver energy with his punches, he has centered himself and concentrated his weight. His feet are glued to the floor for the briefest of interludes, almost too brief to be noticed or capitalized on.

Almost.

"Almost" becomes obvious to my opponent as he feels himself become disconnected from the ground and lifted toward the lights overhead, as he hears the crowd roar. With his tendons and muscles aflame with adrenaline-drenched survival instinct, his hands, a mere second ago clenched, now open and grab desperately at the fence, at the air, at my hunched form, which is hard at work, in the process of completing the mission of throwing him to the ground. And not just throwing him down, but successfully acquiring a solid, inescapable position, utilizing leverage, weight, and geometry to form a mechanism that keeps him down.

An old wrestling coach of mine once told me something brilliant, and it applies to every fight I've won and, sadly, every fight that I've lost: "Chael, you can tell when a guy breaks." And you *can*, even (nay, especially) when it's you.

But this time it's *not* me. And as I concentrate my full weight upon him, as I consolidate and arrange the physical forces that portend his destruction, I feel him break. It's not a real big thing, but once you've felt it or done it, it's unmistakable. Just a fleeting second of semi-relaxation as his body tells his mind, "I gave *you* a chance to win. It's now up to *me* to survive."

Behavioral scientists in France coined a term that applies to circumstances like this when the world doesn't operate the way you thought it did—*l'idée fixe*, or "fixed idea." It's why you feel a little sense of weirdness, a sense of something being out of place, when you walk up to a set of nonfunctioning escalator stairs. There's absolutely *no* difference in the physical architecture of a set of escalator stairs or regular stairs—platform, riser, platform, riser—but it feels a little peculiar to *walk* up escalator stairs because your mind, through experience, has created a mental trellis that your behaviors grow on. Your brain erects a ladder of symbols that it instructs your body to climb, and when that ladder functions in a nontraditional manner, we freeze. So my opponent's body, accustomed to being upright and active, with an able, experienced, and tested captain (his *mind*) at the helm, has now been waylaid and dragged into the shallows by a junta it has no worthwhile defense against; that junta being *what I do better than he does.*

Once he realizes that, there is a moment, that infinitesimal unit of time, when he *breaks.* His body accepts the inevitability of the outcome. It's now like we're two bad actors in a scene, and we've both stolen a peek at the last page of the script and have made an unspoken, unavoidable pact to get to that page as quickly and painlessly as possible in order to save time and avoid mutual embarrassment.

And so, when that moment comes, I take advantage. But not in my usual way—not by using technique, position, and conditioning to slowly usher my opponent to his loss, almost Socratically allowing my actions to ask his body questions, which it answers itself, drawing ever closer to solution. Nope. That was the *old* Chael. The *new* Chael has no time to lose. I think back to a line I heard from a from a dear friend of mine in New York, a man in a very dangerous, physically demanding line of work. I remember asking him how he adjusted to the demands of his profession, and its attendant risks, as he got older. He told me, "ChaCha, when Nolan Ryan, the best fastball pitcher in the history of the game, got older, he actually had a better curveball than fastball." So now comes the curveball. No long, drawn-out, ground-and-pound. No more emulating John Henry and delivering countless hammer strikes. I've got guys on my side, guys who are teaching me, and I am *learning.*

Ready to get out of here, opponent?

Let.

Me.

Help.

So we make a deal.

The submission is on, and tight. Like the pronouncement of every hack actor on the cardboard bridge of a fake spaceship, *resistance is futile.*

I don't hold submissions any longer than I hold grudges.

Tap. Great. We're done.

OK, c'mere ya big lug. Great fight. You got nothin' to be ashamed of.

You and me got more in common than we got to fight about. We both engage in the complete destruction of ourselves for the entertainment of strangers. We go about it in different ways—but *you* need *me*, and *I* need *you*, like the devil says to God in *Paradise Lost*.

But for right now my paradise isn't lost—it's *found*. Here, in the middle of the Octagon, amid the screaming hordes of MMA fans, the energy radiating around the building like a cloud of electrified argon gas, my adrenaline and endorphins sharpening my senses to a degree that only people who engage in high-risk activities like MMA fighting, or its real, and truly deadly template, actual warfare, ever feel.

Here comes Rogan. Now I have to speak. My parasympathetic nervous system stretches my vocal cords like one of Jerry Garcia's banjo strings as he and Grisman tune up for "Foggy Mountain Breakdown," so if I don't calm down and concentrate, I'm going to sound like a hick version of Minnie Mouse. But concentrate I must; I'm a fighter, and even though I just *won*, my work is far from done. I now have to convince all the fans to tell my bosses to let me fight again, real soon, for the championship. So that's what I'm going to do. But taking the microphone from Rogan is like grabbing a crack pipe away from Charlie Sheen; he's got a white-knuckle grip on the damned thing, so I hafta crane my head into his personal space to wedge in a filibuster for my next job. Jesus, Joe. Let the damned thing *go*. I worked on this material for *weeks*. Is it *glued* to your hand?

So I give my pitch, I say my piece. Rogan's like Sinatra. He gives you your solo, and then he wisely snatches the microphone back before you start playing the same notes and boring the paying customers into watching *The Black Swan* on IFC. And then, an inspector in a dodgy blazer unceremoniously throws me, and my ecstatic functionaries, out of the cage, so two other guys can get in there and realize their dreams or have them crushed.

My Enemy Is Vanquished—Now What?

I'm going to give you one final peek behind the curtain, boys and girls.

Nothing would please me more than to have a big finish, like Beethoven or a successful porn star, but, alas, of all the things I owe you for buying this book, the last one should be a vivid depiction of the postfight scene.

Off to the dressing room area backstage. Followed, and watched carefully, by the same inspector who threw me out of the ring a few moments ago. No dressing room, shower, or privacy just yet. There's the little matter of the postfight urine sample. This ritual has a rather desperate relevance for Ol' ChaCha, as you can imagine, in light of the circumstances in which I found myself in California. But here we go. I just sweated enough liquid out to float a battleship on, and now I have to find just a little more for that plastic jar with my name on it.

Then it's off to the showers, where I begin to experience the inevitable adrenaline dump. It starts as a sense of quiet satisfaction, a kind of counterfeit serenity. I use the word "counterfeit" after much reflection and consideration, since I know the few moments of the dump are simply a chemically-induced respite from the restlessness, anxiety, and dissatisfaction that define most of my life, and which defines the lives of fighters in general. The whole "Peaceful Warrior/I Consider This a Sport/I Have No Anger" act is a complete fraud, a construct; it is as artificial as a Mardi Gras parade float, and just as fragile.

Peaceful people do peaceful work.

Peaceful people dig wells in third-world villages.

Peaceful people become Doctors Without Borders.

Fighters *fight* for a *reason*.

If you have no anger, if you have no rage, it is next to impossible to fight successfully against people who *do* have anger and rage.

All you fighters out there playing that "nice guy" angle. …

You can fake the funk all you want to get sponsorships. You can give the fans that whole "aw shucks" bit, and smile like a bashful schoolchild taking his class picture. But in your head, you're just as much of a beast as I am.

I can't tell you why. Nobody beat me with a belt or held my hand on a hot light bulb or starved me when I was a child. Nobody, and no thing, or event, or syndrome made me fight. But I was *compelled* to fight. I was drawn to combat, even as a child. I wasn't a bully or a terror in school. I was just someone who made a decision, based on factors that I felt without understanding, to *fight*. So fight I did.

Which is why the time postfight can be the worst. Imagine doing what you're best at, what makes you feel most alive, only twice a year. Imagine being a great chef, and being allowed to cook only two dinners a year. Imagine being a falcon, genetically engineered for flight and hunting, and having only two mice to swoop down on each year. Think about standing in that kitchen full of cooking implements, sharp knives, colanders, and copper skillets, and watching them lie there unused. Or imagine yourself perched high up in your favorite tree with a perfect view of the forest floor, as you watch mice and voles scurry about, and not being able to swoop down to grab them.

Imagine the sense of furious, helpless waiting for that chance to cook or hunt or fight.

Now consider this:

Of those two meals you get to cook, or those two mice you get to hunt, imagine burning the roast or missing the mouse.

That sense of helpless, bitter rage is what consumes you when you lose a fight. You get only so many chances to fight, and winning is great. But winning means waiting to fight again, which is torture for someone who fights.

But losing. …

Well, losing a fight is simply the worst feeling. It is a curse and a torture, a sense of time wasted, opportunity squandered, and future prospects dimmed.

It represents the possibility of a financial downturn, but any fighter who tells you that losing affects him because of its economic impact is a damned liar.

Losing a fight hurts because it affects your ability to fight in the future.

And for me, and people like me, fighting isn't what we *do*; it's who we *are*.